Good Housekeeping

EASY GLUTEN-FREE!

HEALTHY & DELICIOUS RECIPES FOR EVERY MEAL

Caramelized Chili Shrimp Stir-Fry (page 109)

Good Housekeeping
EASY
GLUTEN-FREE!

HEALTHY & DELICIOUS RECIPES FOR EVERY MEAL

HEARST BOOKS
New York

HEARST BOOKS
New York

An Imprint of Sterling Publishing
387 Park Avenue South
New York, NY 10016

ISBN 978-1-61837-176-8

Every effort has been made to ensure that all the
information in this book is accurate. However, due
to differing health conditions, individual medical
histories, and changes in food product ingredients,
the publisher cannot be responsible for any inju-
ries, losses, and/or other damages that may result
from the use of the information in this book.

The information in this book is not meant to take
the place of the advice of your doctor. Before embarking on a gluten-free diet, you are advised to
seek your doctor's counsel to make sure that the
diet plan you choose is right for your particular
needs. Further, this book's mention of products
made by various companies does not imply that
those companies endorse this book.

Library of Congress Cataloging-in-Publication Data

Good Housekeeping easy gluten-free! : healthy
and delicious recipes for every meal.
    p. cm.
  Summary: "Filled with practical information,
including an intro that explains how to discern
whether you need to eat gluten-free, this Good
Housekeeping cookbook shares the essentials of
shopping and cooking with gluten-free ingredients that are easily found in supermarkets. Handy
charts help you avoid hidden gluten in packaged
foods and pantry staples and make it easy to prepare favorite dishes minus the gluten"-- Provided
by publisher.
  ISBN 978-1-58816-870-2 (hardback)
1. Gluten-free diet--Recipes. 2. Celiac disease--
Diet therapy--Recipes. 3. Cookbooks. I. Good
Housekeeping Institute (New York, N.Y.) II. Title:
Easy gluten free!
  RM237.86.G66 2012
  641.3--dc23

                          2011030035

The Good Housekeeping Cookbook Seal guar-
antees that the recipes in this cookbook meet
the strict standards of the Good Housekeeping
Research Institute. The Institute has been a source
of reliable information and a consumer advocate
since 1900, and established its seal of approval in
1909. Every recipe has been triple-tested for ease,
reliability, and great taste.

Distributed in Canada by Sterling Publishing
c/o Canadian Manda Group, 165 Dufferin Street
Toronto, Ontario, Canada M6K 3H6

Distributed in the United Kingdom by GMC
Distribution Services
Castle Place, 166 High Street, Lewes, East Sussex,
England BN7 1XU

Distributed in Australia by Capricorn Link
(Australia) Pty. Ltd.
P.O. Box 704, Windsor, NSW 2756, Australia

For information about custom editions, special
sales, and premium and corporate purchases,
please contact Sterling Special Sales at
800-805-5489 or specialsales@sterlingpublishing.com.

Manufactured in China

2 4 6 8 10 9 7 5 3 1

www.sterlingpublishing.com

CONTENTS

Oven-Baked Macaroni and Cheese (page 150)

FOREWORD

Recently interest in a gluten-free lifestyle and products has soared. Some people have been diagnosed with celiac disease, others have discovered that they or a family member is experiencing sensitivity to gluten. And, yes, there has been a fad of gluten-free dieting as a weight-loss tool. All of those concerned are looking for advice on navigating their way through the grocery store and cooking their favorite foods with gluten-free ingredients.

My own interest in gluten-free products came about when a friend was diagnosed with celiac disease about a decade ago. I researched brands and trolled the supermarket reading labels, finding gluten in everything from chicken broth to candy bars. Suddenly I was on a mission to make delicious gluten-free food, from sauces to stuffing to desserts.

While *Good Housekeeping* doesn't endorse a gluten-free diet for the general population, we want to provide recipes and advice for those who need to be on one. So, we created *Easy Gluten-Free!* to deliver tasty, healthful, gluten-free recipes for breakfasts, lunches, and dinners. Our introduction explores whether you should be following a gluten-free diet; a visit to your doctor is always step number one. Straightforward charts and tips on label reading will help you separate gluten-free ingredients from those that contain gluten.

Then it's on to the recipes, including gluten-free takes on all of your favorites—pasta, stir-fries, barbecue, casseroles, burgers, and even pizza. Because baking gluten-free is a challenge, we provide a recipe for a simple all-purpose flour blend used in our banana bread, muffins, classic cookies, and more. Icons at the end of each recipe identify dishes you can make ahead ⬛ or prepare in 30 minutes or less ◉. Low-cal ☺, heart healthy ♥, and high-fiber ⊕ recipes are indicated, too.

Whether you are eating gluten-free or cooking for someone who is, *Easy Gluten-Free!* aims to take the worry out of gluten-free shopping and eating. So, check our ingredient lists, shop, and start cooking.

SUSAN WESTMORELAND
Food Director, *Good Housekeeping*

LIVING GLUTEN-FREE

You may be opening this book for a variety of reasons. Maybe you're one of the estimated 3 million people in the United States who have been diagnosed with celiac disease. Perhaps you're wondering what's up with all the gluten-free products that can now be found lining the shelves at your local supermarket or popular outlets like Trader Joe's, Whole Foods Market, and even Walmart. Possibly you've seen celebrities touting the benefits of a gluten-free diet—or you've heard friends or extended social circles buzzing with stories about how gluten-free living has made them feel healthier. You may have even heard reports that eating a gluten-free diet can help relieve autism or lead to weight loss. Not all of these claims have been proved. But if gluten-free eating is truly necessary for you, growing numbers of products—along with resources like this book—are making life easier than ever.

One reason gluten-free food has become a booming $2.6 billion market, growing by 30 percent a year (according to the research company Packaged Facts), is that many consumers now think gluten-free foods are healthier and of higher quality than "regular" foods. But only a small percentage of the population actually requires a gluten-free diet to stay healthy. For those people, eliminating wheat and many other grains has sometimes been a hardship marked by difficult restrictions and tasteless, often expensive alternatives. That's where *Good Housekeeping Easy Gluten-Free!* comes in. Here, you'll find a balanced mix of satisfying recipes for every meal, including naturally gluten-free dishes, plus reworks of favorites that substitute

gluten-free grains and flours. These recipes can be the foundation of a healthy, gluten-free diet for those who need it. Does that include you? See "Who Benefits from Gluten-Free?" on page 12 to find out. We'll also offer tips on navigating the grocery store and kitchen for those who must eat gluten-free as a necessity and not a lifestyle choice.

GLUTEN-FREE GUIDELINES

People on a gluten-free diet must avoid many foods, although the good news is that more gluten-free alternative products appear on the market all the time. Here's a balanced look at what's allowed and what's not. Even with this list in hand you'll need to read labels carefully, especially of items in the "may be allowed" category. For tips on some key words to look out for, see "Hidden Gluten on Labels" on page 21.

ALLOWED	MAY BE ALLOWED	NOT ALLOWED
GRAINS, STARCHES, FLOURS		
Amaranth	Flavored and seasoned rice mixes	Barley
Arrowroot		Bran
Bean flours	Oats, oat bran, oat syrup (see "The Story of Oats," page 31)	Bulgur
Buckwheat (pure buckwheat)		Couscous (Moroccan pasta)
Corn (maize)	Rice and corn cereals	Cracked wheat
Flax	Soba noodles (choose 100-percent buckwheat)	Durum flour
Legume flours (garbanzo/ chick pea, lentil, pea)		Einkorn
Millet	Wheat starch (OK if specially processed to remove gluten)	Emmer
Montina (Indian rice grass)		Farina
Nut flours (almond, hazelnut, pecan)		Farro
Potato starch, potato flour		Gluten, gluten flour
Quinoa		Graham flour
Rice (brown, white, basmati, etc.), rice bran, rice polish		Kamut
Sago		Malt, malt extract, malt flavoring
Seed flours (sesame)		Matzoh, matzo, matzoh semolina
Sorghum		Orzo (rice-shaped pasta)
Soy (soya)		Rye
Sweet potato flour		Semolina (durum wheat)
Tapioca (cassava or manioc)		Spelt (also known as dinkel)
Teff (tef)		Triticale
Wild rice		Wheat flour, wheat germ, wheat bran
FRUITS AND VEGETABLES		
Plain fresh, frozen, and unflavored canned fruits and vegetables	Fruits and vegetables frozen or packaged in a sauce	

GLUTEN-FREE GUIDELINES, *continued*

ALLOWED	MAY BE ALLOWED	NOT ALLOWED
DAIRY		
Aged hard cheeses (Swiss, Cheddar, Parmesan, etc.)	Cheese sauces (plain or on frozen vegetables or in frozen dinners)	Malted milk
Buttermilk		Packaged shredded cheeses (grate your own instead)
Cream	Cream cheese	Processed cheeses
Milk	Flavored yogurts	
Plain yogurt	Ice cream	
	Ricotta cheese	
MEATS AND PROTEINS		
Eggs	Canned meat	Seitan
Legumes (beans, chickpeas, lentils, nuts; rinse before using)	Processed meats (meat patties and premade burgers, meat loaf, deli meats, cold cuts, bologna, hot dogs, sausages, imitation crab)	Bouillon cubes
Plain beef, pork, poultry, game, fish, shellfish		
Tofu	Veggie burgers, veggie sausages, veggie nuggets	
	Baked beans	
	Tempeh (may be seasoned with soy sauce)	
READY-MADE CONDIMENTS, SEASONINGS, AND SAUCES		
Apple cider vinegar	Chicken, beef, or vegetable broth	Gravy
Distilled white vinegar		Malt vinegar
Grape or wine/spirit vinegars	Ketchup	Soy sauce
	Mayonnaise	
Plain pickles, relish, olives	Mustard	
Tamari	Salad dressing	
	Worcestershire sauce (gluten-free in the U.S.)	
ALCOHOL		
Distilled alcoholic beverages (brandy, scotch, whiskey, vodka, etc.)	Liqueurs and other flavored alcoholic beverages	Beer
		Malt beverages
Wine		

GLUTEN-FREE GUIDELINES, *continued*

ALLOWED	MAY BE ALLOWED	NOT ALLOWED
OTHER BEVERAGES		
Fruit and vegetable juices Sodas (regular and diet) Unflavored coffees and teas	Coffee-drink flavoring syrups Flavored coffees Flavored herbal teas	
FATS		
Butter Lard Olive oil Shortening Vegetable oil	Margarine 	
SWEETS AND BAKING INGREDIENTS		
Active dry yeast, instant yeast Cornstarch Corn syrup Honey Jam, jelly, marmalade Maple syrup Molasses Nonstick cooking spray made without flour Sugar (white, brown, confectioners') Vanilla (pure)	Baking powder (Rumford, Clabber Girl, Calumet, and Davis brands are gluten-free) Brewer's yeast (nutritional yeast) Chocolate (baking, chocolate chips) Peanut butter (natural peanut butter is gluten-free; sweetened peanut butters may not be gluten-free) Vanilla extract	Barley malt, barley malt syrup Nonstick cooking spray for baking (contains wheat flour) 
SNACK FOODS AND CANDIES		
Plain nuts Plain popcorn 	Chocolates and chocolate bars Plain or flavored potato chips (BBQ, sour cream and onion, etc.) Plain or flavored corn chips	Dry-roasted and flavored nuts such as smoked almonds Licorice, including strawberry-flavored twists

WHAT IS GLUTEN?

A lot of people associate gluten with wheat, but that's only the beginning. Gluten is a protein found in many grains, wheat among them. Although gluten's chemistry can vary from one grain to the next, in the case of wheat, rye, and barley, the particular sequence of amino acids that forms the protein can damage the gastrointestinal tract of some people, even when eaten in small amounts. To avoid this protein and the damage it can wreak, people diagnosed with celiac disease (and others who are sensitive to gluten) must forgo eating gluten-containing foods. The restrictions include many staples—some of which would otherwise be important parts of a healthy diet, such as whole-grain products like breads and pastas. Standard cookies and baked goods are generally off-limits as well, along with products that may contain hidden amounts of gluten, such as French fries, soy sauce, and many other store-bought condiments.

WHO BENEFITS FROM GLUTEN-FREE?

The recipes in this book make it straightforward to follow a gluten-free diet, providing meals that are satisfying, tasty, and absent of gluten proteins. People with celiac disease who need to follow a gluten-free diet to the letter will benefit from these recipes immediately. But for those with gluten sensitivities or wheat allergies, a total commitment to a gluten-free diet may not be necessary, and may even have some drawbacks. Different conditions warrant varying levels of concern about gluten in the diet, and following the recipes in this book can help you avoid gluten to the extent that is right for you. Here are key considerations to weigh when deciding whether to go gluten-free. Before embarking on a gluten-free diet, you should see your doctor (see "Diagnosing Gluten-Related Conditions," page 20).

CELIAC DISEASE SYMPTOMS

Everyone who has celiac disease experiences it slightly differently. Gastrointestinal symptoms are especially common, and celiac disease can easily be mistaken for conditions such as irritable bowel syndrome, Crohn's disease, and gastric ulcers. But some people with celiac disease aren't bothered by GI symptoms at all. Instead, they may suffer from subtle or hard-to-pin-down problems resulting in part from malnutrition. Among the signs to watch for:

- Chronic diarrhea or constipation
- Recurring gas, bloating, or abdominal pain
- Pale grayish, smelly stools that may be oily or fatty
- Weight loss
- Fatigue, perhaps tied to unexplained anemia
- Muscle cramps
- Tingling or numbness in the legs
- Bone or joint pain
- Mouth sores or itchy skin rashes
- Behavioral changes such as irritability or depression

Celiac disease: Sometimes called celiac sprue or gluten-sensitive enteropathy, celiac disease is an autoimmune condition that damages the small intestine. "Autoimmune" means the immune system attacks the body it's meant to protect, for reasons that are still largely mysterious. Celiac disease specifically damages tiny hairlike projections called villi that line the small intestine and absorb nutrients such as vitamins, minerals, fat, and protein from food. When damaged villi are unable to do their job properly, the body eliminates nutrients it needs, leaving sufferers prone to a range of problems, including deficiencies, gastrointestinal troubles, loss of bone density, and complications such as neurological disorders. Gluten triggers these autoimmune attacks, so eating a gluten-free diet is essential for people who want to control this disease and ease their symptoms. The good news is that eating a gluten-free diet can not only control symptoms but reverse damage to the gastrointestinal tract. Most people with celiac disease feel better within days or weeks of beginning a gluten-free diet.

Gluten sensitivity: This condition is poorly understood, and some doctors question whether it even exists. But significant numbers of people seem to suffer symptoms similar to those of celiac disease and get better when they eat a gluten-free diet, yet don't have damage to the intestinal tract or some of the complications of celiac disease. If it acts like celiac disease but isn't, then what is it? In early 2011, researchers at the Center for Celiac Research at the University of Maryland, working with colleagues at Johns Hopkins University and scientists in Italy, announced they'd found the first scientific evidence of a gluten reaction that's real but different than celiac disease. These findings are preliminary, but researchers suggest there may be a spectrum of gluten sensitivity between the opposite extremes of celiac disease on one hand and no reaction at all on the other. The center estimates that 18 million people in the United States—about 6 percent of us—may suffer from gluten sensitivity. As yet, there's no test or set of standards for diagnosing the condition, but it appears that following a gluten-free diet helps. It's essential that you work with your doctor to evaluate any symptoms you may be experiencing, as well as whether a gluten-free diet might be useful. As noted in "Diagnosing Gluten-Related Conditions" on page 20, trying a gluten-free diet without input from a physician can complicate the medical detective work necessary to determine what's causing symptoms.

Wheat allergy: Although a wheat allergy also involves the immune system, it's different than the autoimmune reaction that defines celiac disease. With a wheat allergy, instead of mistaking the body for an enemy, the immune system sees wheat in food as an invader and reacts

the way it does in other allergies—by triggering itchy, watery eyes, nasal congestion, swelling, itching, hives, and, in some severe cases, a dangerous condition known as anaphylaxis that can swell airways and make breathing difficult. Wheat allergy typically shows up in infancy and disappears by age five, so it's not common in adolescents or adults. By eating a gluten-free diet, people with wheat allergies can avoid trigger foods that contain wheat proteins—which are many of the same foods that people with celiac disease need to avoid.

But people who are allergic to wheat may be able to tolerate other types of grain that are no-nos for people with celiac disease, such as barley and rye. (See "Gluten-Free Survival Guide" on page 16 for reasons to be cautious about committing to a 100-percent gluten-free diet.) If you think you or your child has a wheat allergy, check with your doctor to review symptoms, family history of allergy or asthma (which can increase the risk of allergies in general), and details about how and when reactions occur. Your doctor or an allergist may try a combination of diagnostic tools, such as keeping a food diary, eliminating certain foods from the diet, or doing a variety of tests including skin, blood, or food-challenge tests. Medications such as antihistamines or epinephrine may help control symptoms, but your doctor may also recommend shopping for gluten-free foods or using recipes like those in this book to help minimize exposure to wheat products.

Autism: Will following a gluten-free diet help relieve autism? Unfortunately, there's not much evidence for this. Little research has been done on the autism-gluten connection, but one of the most highly regarded studies, released in 2010 by researchers at the University of Rochester, found no improvement in autistic kids without celiac disease who were given a gluten-free, casein-free diet for at least four weeks. The study was small but well controlled, with fourteen children adhering strictly to the diet, then being given gluten- and casein-containing snacks while being monitored for changes in behavior and sleep, attention, activity, and bowel patterns. No significant changes were noted when the children went on or off the diet. Though disappointing, some struggling parents may be reassured that their autistic child won't have to maintain a difficult diet.

Cost: You'll typically pay more for gluten-free products. One study found that gluten-free breads and pasta cost about twice as much

as their wheat-based counterparts. Following our recipe for homemade gluten-free bread on page 49 can help save you money on a basic staple—and fill your house with a homey fresh-baked aroma and flavor you won't get with store-bought breads.

GLUTEN-FREE SURVIVAL GUIDE

People who have already experienced gluten-free living because their health depends on it might scratch their heads at the newfangled popularity of gluten-free food, because they know the diet can be challenging and may actually have some health-related drawbacks. For the veterans, consider the following a refresher with helpful pointers. For those new to a gluten-free diet, here are a number of potential pitfalls that we'll help you work your way through.

Nutrition: Unlike wheat-based products, many gluten-free grain products aren't fortified or enriched, so people eating them may not get enough of key nutrients such as iron, folate, thiamin, and riboflavin. For that reason, experts caution against putting kids on a gluten-free diet unless it will help deal with a medical condition such as celiac disease. (See "Maximizing Nutrition" on page 22 for more on meeting special nutritional needs with gluten-free eating.) Throughout this book, you'll find ingredients and recipes that provide the building blocks for a healthy, well-balanced diet that includes the vitamins and minerals you need even while eliminating gluten.

Weight gain: Think again if you believe following a gluten-free diet will automatically make you as skinny as the svelte celebrities who proclaim the benefits of a gluten-free diet to their fans. Although some people have the impression a gluten-free diet can help with weight loss, the opposite appears more likely. In one study of people with celiac disease who went on a gluten-free diet for two years, 81 percent put on pounds. The example of thin celebrities does suggest one thing, though: Gaining weight with gluten-free isn't inevitable. But it pays to know what you're up against to help manage your intake of calories. People with celiac disease may gain weight because healing the villi of the small intestine means the body can absorb more calories from fat, carbohydrates, and protein. Plus, they may be used to eating relatively large amounts of food without putting on weight—so once absorption improves, pounds

start to stick. Even those without a digestive disorder may be prone to weight gain because gluten-free alternatives often contain more fat and sugar than standard grain-based versions. Since gluten-free foods are often denser in texture, portions may be smaller, which means if you continue eating the serving size you're accustomed to, you'll be overeating. Gluten-free products tend to be low in fiber that would help fill you up and keep you satisfied longer. And they generally have more fast-acting carbs, which can spike blood sugar and make it more difficult to control cravings.

Fortunately, whole foods such as fresh fruits and vegetables, lean sources of protein, and whole grains, are a foundation of both gluten-free and weight-control diets, so if you emphasize eating produce and avoiding packaged foods, you'll have a huge advantage in the battle of the bulge. Bonus: Besides being loaded with vitamins and minerals, fruits, vegetables, and whole grains generally contain lots of fiber to help keep you full. Watching portion sizes with packaged products—especially the array of indulgent gluten-free options now available—is another sensible approach to maintaining a healthy weight while taking advantage of products that are making gluten-free eating more convenient. Experts advise reading product labels not just to find gluten-free information but to keep tabs on serving sizes, fat, and calories.

Eating out: Cooking for yourself is the best option, but most people find themselves heading to a restaurant at some point. The good news is that you're increasingly likely to find establishments that are sensitive to your needs—and capable of fulfilling them—even if you have celiac disease. The National Restaurant Association, in its 2011 annual poll of members, ranked "gluten-free/food allergy conscious" number eight on its list of twenty hottest trends. "Ancient grains," including gluten-free quinoa and millet, check in as the fourth-hottest ingredient type. Vegan and vegetarian restaurants are good bets, but even chain restaurants like Chili's, Olive Garden, Outback, and Carrabba's have

offered gluten-free sections in their menus (although they don't always guarantee that foods haven't been contaminated by gluten-containing food on the grill). Call ahead to see how amenable the restaurant is to special diets and ensure what you eat is actually gluten-free. Check to see if menus are available online and scout for gluten-free dishes. When you arrive, explain in simple terms to the restaurant workers what you can't eat. (You might find the restaurant crew more amenable if you make your first visit at an off-peak hour, when they have more time to listen.) Use a pleasant, informative tone, but don't be shy about asking how food is prepared.

Cross-contamination: Whether making food in your home, eating restaurant-prepared dishes, or buying gluten-free bulk items like flour, grains, or nuts, you run the risk of gluten-free items becoming contaminated by contact with gluten-containing surfaces or substances. Don't buy bulk items from bins, where scoops can easily be moved from one bin to the next and grain dust containing gluten can float through the air and land in gluten-free products. At home, it would be ideal to create a completely gluten-free kitchen, but if other family members don't have celiac disease or gluten sensitivity, it may be difficult to completely ban regular foods. If that's the case, be sure to dedicate areas of your counter to gluten-free food preparation (or be sure to thoroughly wash hands and surfaces as you alternate between gluten-free and gluten-containing food preparation) and make sure cutting boards used for gluten-free foods aren't used for anything else. Set aside a toaster or toaster oven exclusively for gluten-free products and use clean gluten-free utensils (label or color-code them so everyone knows what's what). Be especially careful to have separate colanders, with their tiny, difficult-to-clean holes, for straining foods like pasta. And encourage family members, guests, and restaurant cooks to follow these guidelines as well. When buying packaged products, be aware that contamination can occur in food-handling factories, so it's best to buy specifically gluten-free products or check labels for warnings that an item may have been handled with machines that have contact with gluten- or wheat-containing material. (For more, see "Buying Gluten-Free" on page 22.)

GLUTEN-FREE FOODS THAT ARE GOOD SOURCES OF FIBER

Avoiding off-limits foods doesn't have to leave you fiber-deprived. Here's a look at naturally gluten-free foods that contain 3 grams of fiber or more per serving, which makes them good sources or fiber according to the USDA. Note that the recommended amount of fiber per day is 25 to 30 grams a day for women and 30 to 38 grams for men, according to the Institute of Medicine, which establishes the nation's Dietary Reference Intakes.

GRAINS AND BEANS (½ CUP COOKED)

Buckwheat groats

Garbanzo, kidney, black, white, pinto, adzuki, lima, navy beans

Lentils

Soybeans (edamame)

Split peas

NUTS AND SEEDS (1 OUNCE)

Almonds

Flaxseed

Hazelnuts (filberts)

Pecans

Pistachios

Sesame seeds

Sunflower seeds

VEGETABLES AND STARCHES (½ CUP COOKED)

Artichokes

Peas

Sweet potato (with skin)

Winter squash (especially acorn)

FRUITS (½ CUP RAW)

Raspberries

DIAGNOSING GLUTEN-RELATED CONDITIONS

The best way to know how you'll benefit from a gluten-free diet is to get a proper evaluation—and potentially, a celiac diagnosis—from your doctor before you start. Going gluten-free before checking in with a physician could handicap a diagnosis for a number of reasons. First, tests won't discover clear evidence of celiac disease if damage to the intestines has already been repaired or erased by eating gluten-free, so your doctor could miss the disease. Second, because celiac disease shares symptoms with many other problems, a doctor who doesn't find evidence of celiac disease could go on to pinpoint a different condition and thus misdiagnose you. And third, monitoring what happens in your gut both before and after you begin a gluten-free diet can confirm whether you have celiac disease or shed light on what's going on in your system.

Your doctor may use a number of tests and procedures to detect or rule out celiac disease. Among them are blood tests that look for specific antibodies found in people with celiac disease, an endoscopic biopsy of the small intestine to check out damage to the villi, and possibly a visual check using a camera pill that takes pictures as it travels through your small intestine.

GEARING UP FOR GLUTEN-FREE

The beauty of a gluten-free diet for those who can truly benefit from it is that this lifestyle change can have life-changing effects—without risky surgeries or pricey medications and the side effects they bring. The hardest part may be changing ingrained habits—both for you and your family. Here's a checklist of steps that can help make it easier to go on a gluten-free diet and stick with it:

• Get as much information as you can about celiac conditions and a gluten-free diet from your doctor, reputable websites, books like this, and other people who have experience with conditions related to gluten-free eating.

• Check your pantry for favorite foods that may already be gluten-free. Use our "Gluten-Free Guidelines" on page 9 as a checklist.

• Get to know what you can and can't eat—and where gluten may be hidden (see "Hidden Gluten on Labels," opposite).

HIDDEN GLUTEN ON LABELS

When shopping, check labels on ready-made and processed foods such as soups, gravies, marinated meats, condiments, and more that contain emulsifiers, flavorings, hydrolyzed proteins, seasonings, stabilizers, and starches from unidentified sources. Here are some key words to look out for, as they may indicate that gluten is present. If in doubt, contact the company's customer-service center.

- Barley malt extract or barley malt flavoring
- Caramel coloring
- Dextrin
- Gravy
- Hydrolyzed wheat, plant, or vegetable proteins (HVP indicates hydrolyzed vegetable proteins)
- Malt (it's generally gluten-free if made from corn)
- Modified food starch/food starch (it's generally gluten-free if made from rice, corn, or potato)
- Roux
- Soy sauce
- Textured vegetable protein (TVP)
- Vegetable gum (except the following gluten-free options: carob bean gum, cellulose gum, guar gum, locust bean gum, xanthan gum, gum arabic, gum aracia, gum tragacanth, and vegetable starch)
- Wheat flour or wheat gluten

- Plan meals around gluten-free foods and ingredients, starting with recipes such as those in this book.
- Take steps to make your kitchen gluten-free or set aside areas where you can safely prepare gluten-free foods.
- Travel the perimeter of your grocery store, where fresh produce and other naturally gluten-free foods tend to be stocked, and note just how many options already exist there.
- Develop skills for identifying and avoiding gluten, such as label reading, knowing hidden sources, and avoiding cross-contamination. (See the item on cross-contamination on page 18 and "Buying Gluten-Free" on page 22.)

- Form a team of medical partners—your doctor, nutritionist, pharmacist, and other professionals who contribute to your care, such as your dentist or psychologist.
- Establish a system of support and resources and consider joining a local or national support group.

MAXIMIZING NUTRITION

Nutrient shortfalls due to poor absorption can be a major issue with celiac disease, and people on a gluten-free diet may need to take special steps to get enough of certain nutrients, especially those normally supplied by fortified grains. Work with your doctor and dietitian to make sure you're getting enough iron, thiamin, riboflavin, niacin, and folate, and ask for recommendations on supplements if you're falling short. It's important to get your doctor's advice on the right amounts for you, because your ability to absorb nutrients may be different from someone else's. If you have low bone density (a common issue with celiac disease), your doctor may also recommend a supplement of vitamin D, which works with calcium to build strong bones. Have your team ascertain your fiber status as well: Because grains are restricted, people on a gluten-free diet often need to consume more fiber-rich foods. We make it easier: The recipes in this book feature a special icon that indicates high fiber content—those recipes containing 5 grams or more of fiber per serving.

BUYING GLUTEN-FREE

Gluten-free labeling is still a work in progress: The Food and Drug Administration has proposed a gluten-free labeling rule, and efforts to implement it are gathering steam. Proposed regulations may require foods labeled gluten-free to contain less than 20 parts per million (ppm) of gluten, currently the smallest amount that can reliably be detected. Proposed terms that would be allowed—which you may already find on packages—include "gluten-free,"

"without gluten," "no gluten," and "free of gluten." Until a formal definition of "gluten-free" is in place, the FDA allows the above terms to be used on products as long as they are not misleading. As of fall 2011, labeling standards are still voluntary but may contain advisories such as "Produced in a plant that also produces products made with wheat" to indicate possible cross-contamination.

In the meantime, avoid foods whose labels indicate they contain wheat, rye, barley, and, for some people, oats (see "The Story of Oats" on page 31, along with "Hidden Gluten on Labels" on page 21 for other ingredients and terms to watch for.) To help make cooking easier for you, we provide gluten-free product suggestions within many of our recipes, though you may want to do some taste-testing to find the brands with the flavor and texture you like best. Cooking—and especially baking—from scratch offers you the most control over the ingredients that go into your food. We offer a simple recipe for a basic all-purpose flour blend on page 25 that uses gluten-free flours like the ones shown below—along with suggestions for premixed flour blends if you're looking for a shortcut. Tip: Not all potentially contaminated products are foods. You could also inadvertently ingest gluten in products such as lipstick and lip balms, toothpaste, food additives, and medications or supplements that use gluten as a binding agent.

GLUTEN-FREE BAKING TIPS

Baking is the biggest challenge for people on a gluten-free diet, but our recipes use a premixed gluten-free flour mix (see opposite) to keep baking as easy as possible—not to mention fun. Our buckwheat pancakes, banana bread, and muffins make for satisfying breakfasts while our gluten-free cookie options—and the flourless chocolate cake—will keep everyone happy come dessert. Our homemade sandwich bread will help you avoid the cost of expensive—and often less palatable—commercial gluten-free breads, but if you're interested in good ready-made products, check out "Commercial Gluten-Free Breads" on page 45. As you practice and learn more about the properties of gluten-free ingredients, baking can become a forte instead of a frustration. Here are a few tips to get you started:

- Store ingredients in a gluten-free pantry to avoid cross-contamination.
- Some brands of vanilla extract contain gluten. If you want to avoid label-reading, use pure vanilla extract.
- Avoid overbeating egg whites, which can make them more difficult to mix into a batter and affect the volume and structure of the finished product—for example, causing cakes to flop.
- Prevent gluten-free batter from sticking by greasing surfaces with shortening and dusting with rice flour. Even easier: Line pans with parchment paper.
- Use a whisk for mixing to give gluten-free ingredients extra aeration and lift.

ALL-PURPOSE FLOUR BLEND

This gluten-free flour blend is used in multiple baked goods in this book—from pizza crust to cookies—so it's well worth the effort to mix up a batch and keep it on hand. For a shortcut, you can swap in a commercial all-purpose flour blend: Arrowhead Mills, Bob's Red Mill, and Gluten Free Pantry brands all offer gluten-free options. The ingredients vary so they'll yield different results. Experiment until you find a brand you like.

ACTIVE TIME: 5 MINUTES · **TOTAL TIME:** 5 MINUTES
MAKES: 6 CUPS

2 CUPS SORGHUM FLOUR (SEE TIP)	1 CUP TAPIOCA FLOUR
1½ CUPS POTATO STARCH	1 CUP CORN FLOUR

In large bowl, whisk sorghum flour, potato starch, tapioca flour, and corn flour until thoroughly blended. Store in an airtight container up to 1 week.

TIP Sorghum flour, potato starch, and tapioca flour are available at health-food stores or health-oriented supermarkets such as Whole Foods. If you have trouble locating them, ask your local health food store to order them or purchase them online.

EACH ½ CUP: ABOUT 230 CALORIES | 4G PROTEIN | 53G CARBOHYDRATE
1G TOTAL FAT (0G SATURATED FAT) | 4G FIBER | 0MG CHOLESTEROL | 0MG SODIUM

BREAKFASTS & BRUNCHES

Breakfast for most people is a one-note meal: cereal, played over and over. The fact that some staples of a traditional breakfast (including toast) aren't friendly to gluten-free eating is an opportunity in disguise.

Our wide array of gluten-free options provides a necessary burst of day-starting energy, but also breaks you out of a top-of-the-morning rut. For busy weekdays, fix-it-fast options include a smoothie made with a healthy blend of yogurt and berries that you can whip up in little more time than it takes to pour milk on cereal. When you have more time on weekends, you can prepare some truly delectable kick-offs to your day. These include our comforting Potato-Crusted Quiche, which boasts a delicious shredded potato crust that's entirely gluten-free, and Huevos Rancheros, an easy, zesty brunch option featuring corn tortillas that will satisfy everyone at the table. Traditional A.M. ingredients like eggs and buckwheat combine easily with a variety of other gluten-free ingredients to create new classics your grandma might envy, like pancakes, muffins, and banana bread. You'll even find a new take on an old tune with our hazelnut-honey granola—bake a batch in the oven and store it for a familiar cereal-and-milk opener to your day.

Crustless Tomato-Ricotta Pie (page 34)

POMEGRANATE-BERRY SMOOTHIE

Berries and pomegranates are loaded with heart-healthy antioxidants.

TOTAL TIME: 5 MINUTES

MAKES: 2 CUPS OR 1 SERVING

½ CUP POMEGRANATE JUICE, CHILLED

½ CUP PLAIN LOW-FAT YOGURT (SEE TIP)

1 CUP FROZEN MIXED BERRIES

1 TEASPOON HONEY

In blender, combine juice, yogurt, berries, and honey and blend until mixture is smooth. Pour into a tall glass.

TIP Flavored yogurts may include additives that contain gluten. Opt for plain yogurt and add a sweetener, such as honey or agave nectar, or a flavoring, such as vanilla, if you like.

EACH SERVING: ABOUT 260 CALORIES | 6G PROTEIN | 52G CARBOHYDRATE | 2G TOTAL FAT (1G SATURATED) | 5G FIBER | 8MG CHOLESTEROL | 110MG SODIUM ♥ ♥ ♥

BANANA–PEANUT BUTTER SMOOTHIE

This yummy breakfast drink will keep you satisfied until lunchtime.

TOTAL TIME: 5 MINUTES

MAKES: 1½ CUPS OR 1 SERVING

1 SMALL RIPE BANANA, CUT IN HALF

½ CUP SOY MILK

1 TEASPOON NATURAL CREAMY PEANUT BUTTER

3 ICE CUBES

In blender, combine banana, soy milk, peanut butter, and ice, and blend until mixture is smooth. Pour into a tall glass.

EACH SERVING: ABOUT 260 CALORIES | 6G PROTEIN | 52G CARBOHYDRATE | 2G TOTAL FAT (1G SATURATED) | 5G FIBER | 8MG CHOLESTEROL | 110MG SODIUM ♥ ♥ ♥

HAZELNUT AND FRUIT GRANOLA

This scrumptious combination of toasty nuts, old-fashioned oats, and sweetly chewy dried fruit may be enjoyed straight from the container, spooned over plain yogurt, or with a splash of milk. However, before you prepare this recipe, read "The Story of Oats," opposite, and choose only oats that are labeled "gluten-free."

ACTIVE TIME: 10 MINUTES · **TOTAL TIME:** 55 MINUTES
MAKES: 10 CUPS OR 20 SERVINGS

½ CUP HONEY OR AGAVE NECTAR

⅓ CUP VEGETABLE OIL

1½ TEASPOONS VANILLA EXTRACT (McCORMICK, SPICE ISLANDS, AND DURKEE BRANDS ARE GLUTEN-FREE)

½ TEASPOON GROUND CINNAMON

4 CUPS OLD-FASHIONED GLUTEN-FREE OATS, SUCH AS BOB'S RED MILL OR DENNETT'S BRANDS, UNCOOKED

1 CUP FLAKED SWEETENED COCONUT

1 CUP SLICED ALMONDS (4 OUNCES)

1 CUP HAZELNUTS, CHOPPED (4 OUNCES)

¼ CUP FLAXSEEDS

¼ CUP PUMPKIN SEEDS (PEPITAS)

1 CUP DRIED TART CHERRIES

1 CUP DRIED CALIMYRNA FIGS, STEMS REMOVED, CHOPPED

1 CUP DRIED APRICOTS, CHOPPED

1 Preheat oven to 300°F.

2 In large bowl, whisk honey, oil, vanilla, and cinnamon until blended. Add oats, coconut, nuts, flaxseeds, and pumpkin seeds; stir until coated.

3 Divide mixture between two 15½" by 10½" jelly-roll pans; spread evenly.

4 Bake oat mixture until golden brown, 45 to 50 minutes, stirring twice during baking. Cool completely in pans on wire racks.

5 In large bowl, toss cooled oat mixture with cherries, figs, and apricots. Store in tightly covered container at room temperature for up to 1 week. For storage up to 3 weeks, and to keep granola crunchy, spoon oat mixture into one container and cherries, figs, and apricots into another. Mix together when ready to use.

EACH ½-CUP SERVING: ABOUT 270 CALORIES | 5G PROTEIN | 37G CARBOHYDRATE 13G TOTAL FAT (2G SATURATED) | 5G FIBER | 0MG CHOLESTEROL | 5MG SODIUM ♥ ⓥ ▤

THE STORY OF OATS

Are oats gluten-free? That remains an open question. Though oats were once considered a problem for people with celiac disease, recent research suggests a lot of people who can't tolerate gluten can handle oats just fine. But other studies find that most oat products are contaminated with mixtures of wheat, barley, and rye, due to processing at plants that also handle gluten-containing grains.

A small number of people may, in fact, have an immune reaction to oats. As a result, organizations such as the Celiac Sprue Association say oats can't be considered risk free. Some companies have now started offering pure, uncontaminated oats that are processed in dedicated plants, and most people with celiac disease or gluten sensitivities can probably eat these safely, though you should check with your doctor first.

If you're newly diagnosed with celiac disease, gradually introduce oats from dedicated gluten-free processors once symptoms are under control, limiting yourself to no more than 50 uncooked grams of oats per day (a little more than ½ cup rolled oats or ¼ cup steel-cut oats), according to the Celiac Disease Center at Beth Israel Deaconess Medical Center in Boston. Children should be allowed about half that amount.

HUEVOS RANCHEROS

Fast and flavorful, these Mexican-inspired baked eggs are ideal for brunch. Spice up this dish with a drizzle of your favorite hot sauce. Use only corn tortillas made from 100-percent corn; see "Commercial Gluten-Free Breads" on page 45 for details.

TOTAL TIME: 25 MINUTES

MAKES: 4 MAIN-DISH SERVINGS

1 TABLESPOON VEGETABLE OIL	¼ CUP LOOSELY PACKED FRESH CILANTRO LEAVES, CHOPPED
1 MEDIUM ONION, FINELY CHOPPED	
2 GARLIC CLOVES, CRUSHED WITH GARLIC PRESS	¼ TEASPOON SALT
	1 TABLESPOON BUTTER
1 TABLESPOON CHIPOTLE SAUCE OR OTHER HOT SAUCE, PLUS ADDITIONAL FOR SERVING	4 LARGE EGGS
	4 (6-INCH) GLUTEN-FREE CORN TORTILLAS, SUCH AS CHI-CHI'S OR MISSION BRANDS, WARMED
1 TEASPOON GROUND CUMIN	
1 CAN (28 OUNCES) TOMATOES IN JUICE, DRAINED AND CHOPPED	1 AVOCADO, SLICED (OPTIONAL)
1 CAN (15 TO 19 OUNCES) BLACK BEANS, RINSED AND DRAINED	

1 In 4-quart saucepan, heat oil over medium heat until hot. Add onion and garlic and cook 8 minutes or until beginning to brown. Stir in chipotle sauce and cumin; cook 30 seconds, stirring. Add tomatoes; cover and cook 3 minutes to blend flavors, stirring occasionally. Stir in beans, half of cilantro, and salt; heat through, about 3 minutes, stirring occasionally.

2 Meanwhile, in 12-inch nonstick skillet, melt butter over medium heat. Crack eggs, one at a time, and drop into skillet. Cover skillet and cook eggs 4 to 5 minutes or until whites are set and yolks reach desired doneness.

3 Place tortillas on four dinner plates; top each with 1 egg. Sprinkle with remaining cilantro. Serve with avocado slices and additional hot sauce, if you like.

EACH SERVING: ABOUT 315 CALORIES | 15G PROTEIN | 42G CARBOHYDRATE | 12G TOTAL FAT (3G SATURATED) | 10G FIBER | 213MG CHOLESTEROL | 765MG SODIUM ♥ ☺ ⊛

CRUSTLESS TOMATO-RICOTTA PIE

Serve this delicious cross between a frittata and a quiche for brunch or dinner. Try this simple pie with a couple tablespoons of chopped fresh oregano or a handful of chopped fresh dill in place of the basil. For photo, see page 26.

ACTIVE TIME: 20 MINUTES · TOTAL TIME: 55 MINUTES

MAKES: 6 MAIN-DISH SERVINGS

1   CONTAINER (15 OUNCES) PART-SKIM RICOTTA CHEESE (SARGENTO BRAND IS GLUTEN-FREE)

4   LARGE EGGS

¼   CUP FRESHLY GRATED PECORINO-ROMANO CHEESE

½   TEASPOON SALT

⅛   TEASPOON COARSELY GROUND BLACK PEPPER

¼   CUP LOW-FAT (1%) MILK

1   TABLESPOON CORNSTARCH (SEE TIP)

½   CUP LOOSELY PACKED FRESH BASIL LEAVES, CHOPPED

½   CUP LOOSELY PACKED FRESH MINT LEAVES, CHOPPED

1   POUND RIPE TOMATOES (3 MEDIUM), THINLY SLICED

1   Preheat oven to 375°F. In large bowl, whisk ricotta, eggs, Romano, salt, and pepper until blended.

2   In measuring cup, stir milk and cornstarch until smooth; whisk into cheese mixture. Stir in basil and mint.

3   Pour mixture into nonstick 10-inch skillet with oven-safe handle. Arrange tomatoes on top, overlapping slices if necessary. Bake pie 35 to 40 minutes or until lightly browned on top, set around edge, and puffed at center. Let stand 5 minutes before serving.

TIP Most cornstach is gluten-free, but read the label to make sure no wheat is added. Arrowroot can be used as a thickener instead, if you prefer, as can glutinous rice flour, potato flour, and many bean flours.

EACH SERVING: ABOUT 190 CALORIES | 15G PROTEIN | 10G CARBOHYDRATE | 10G TOTAL FAT (5G SATURATED) | 2G FIBER | 165MG CHOLESTEROL | 380MG SODIUM ☺

SOUTH-OF-THE-BORDER VEGETABLE HASH

A savory combination of classic hash ingredients (without the meat) gets a new flavor twist from kidney beans, cilantro, and the zing of fresh lime.

ACTIVE TIME: 20 MINUTES · **TOTAL TIME:** 50 MINUTES
MAKES: 4 MAIN-DISH SERVINGS

3   LARGE YUKON GOLD POTATOES (1½ POUNDS), CUT INTO ¾-INCH CHUNKS

2   TABLESPOONS OLIVE OIL

1   LARGE ONION (12 OUNCES), CUT INTO ¼-INCH DICE

1   MEDIUM RED PEPPER, CUT INTO ¼-INCH-WIDE STRIPS

3   GARLIC CLOVES, CRUSHED WITH GARLIC PRESS

2   TEASPOONS GROUND CUMIN

¾   TEASPOON SALT

1   CAN (15 TO 19 OUNCES) RED KIDNEY OR BLACK BEANS, RINSED AND DRAINED

2   TABLESPOONS CHOPPED FRESH CILANTRO

ACCOMPANIMENTS: PLAIN YOGURT, LIME WEDGES, SALSA, AND WARMED GLUTEN-FREE CORN TORTILLAS (OPTIONAL)

1 In 3-quart saucepan, place potato chunks and enough *water* to cover; heat to boiling over high heat. Reduce heat to low; cover and simmer until potatoes are almost tender, about 5 minutes; drain well.

2 Meanwhile, in nonstick 12-inch skillet, heat oil over medium heat until hot. Add onion, red pepper, garlic, cumin, and salt and cook 10 minutes, stirring occasionally. Add potatoes and cook, turning occasionally, until vegetables are lightly browned, about 5 minutes longer. Stir in beans and cook until heated through, 2 minutes longer. Sprinkle with cilantro.

3 Serve hash with yogurt, lime wedges, salsa, and tortillas, if you like.

EACH SERVING: ABOUT 360 CALORIES | 12G PROTEIN | 63G CARBOHYDRATE | 8G TOTAL FAT (1G SATURATED) | 13G FIBER | 0MG CHOLESTEROL | 625MG SODIUM ☺ ❂ ▥

POTATO-CRUSTED QUICHE

A white flour and butter crust is not a requirement for quiche. Enjoy this clever gluten-free twist, which features a shredded potato crust flecked with green onions.

ACTIVE TIME: 20 MINUTES · **TOTAL TIME:** 40 MINUTES
MAKES: 4 MAIN-DISH SERVINGS

---

4   LARGE EGGS

1   LARGE EGG WHITE

1⅔ CUP LOW-FAT (1%) MILK

¼   TEASPOON SALT

⅛   TEASPOON GROUND BLACK PEPPER

4   OUNCES HAM, CUT INTO ¼-INCH PIECES

1½ POUNDS POTATOES, PEELED AND SHREDDED

2   GREEN ONIONS, CHOPPED

2   TABLESPOONS OLIVE OIL

2   OUNCES SWISS CHEESE, SHREDDED (KRAFT NATURAL SHREDDED SWISS CHEESE IS GLUTEN-FREE)

2   PLUM TOMATOES, THINLY SLICED

FRESH FLAT-LEAF PARSLEY LEAVES AND SNIPPED FRESH CHIVES, FOR GARNISH

1   Preheat oven to 375°F.

2   In large bowl, with wire whisk, blend eggs, egg white, milk, ⅛ teaspoon salt, and pepper. Stir in ham.

3   Place potatoes in large fine-mesh sieve. With hands, squeeze out as much liquid as possible. Transfer to large bowl and toss with green onions and remaining ⅛ teaspoon salt.

4   Heat 12-inch well-seasoned plain or enamel-coated cast-iron skillet on medium-high until hot. Add oil and heat until very hot, brushing to evenly coat bottom and side. Add potatoes; with rubber spatula, quickly spread in thin, even layer over bottom and up side to rim, gently pressing potatoes against pan to form crust. Patch holes by using spatula to spread potatoes over them. Cook 3 minutes or until browned. Pour in egg mixture, then sprinkle Swiss cheese evenly over top.

5   Bake 15 to 20 minutes or until a knife inserted in center comes out clean. Decoratively arrange tomato slices on top. Garnish with parsley and chives. Use thin spatula to release sides of crust from pan, then cut into wedges to serve.

EACH SERVING: ABOUT 425 CALORIES | 23G PROTEIN | 39G CARBOHYDRATE | 20G TOTAL FAT (6G SATURATED) | 4G FIBER | 253MG CHOLESTEROL | 660MG SODIUM ☺

BUCKWHEAT PANCAKES

Buckwheat flour adds a wonderful nutty flavor to these buttermilk pancakes. Because it contains more of the whole grain, keep stored, tightly covered, in the refrigerator to keep it from going rancid.

TOTAL TIME: 30 MINUTES
MAKES: ABOUT 14 PANCAKES

½ CUP ALL-PURPOSE FLOUR BLEND (PAGE 25)
½ CUP BUCKWHEAT FLOUR
1 TABLESPOON SUGAR
2 TEASPOONS BAKING POWDER
½ TEASPOON BAKING SODA
¼ TEASPOON SALT
1¼ CUPS BUTTERMILK
3 TABLESPOONS BUTTER, MELTED AND COOLED
1 LARGE EGG, LIGHTLY BEATEN
VEGETABLE OIL FOR BRUSHING PAN

1 In large bowl, combine flours, sugar, baking powder, baking soda, and salt. Add buttermilk, butter, and egg; stir just until flour is moistened.

2 Heat griddle or 12-inch skillet over medium-low heat until drop of water sizzles when sprinkled on hot surface; brush lightly with oil. Pour batter by scant ¼ cups onto hot griddle, making 2 or 3 pancakes at a time. Cook until tops are bubbly and edges look dry, 2 to 3 minutes. With wide spatula, turn pancakes and cook until undersides brown, 2 to 3 minutes longer. Transfer to platter; keep warm.

3 Repeat with remaining batter, brushing griddle with more oil as needed.

EACH PANCAKE: ABOUT 80 CALORIES | 2G PROTEIN | 8G CARBOHYDRATE | 4G TOTAL FAT (2G SATURATED) | 1G FIBER | 21MG CHOLESTEROL | 215MG SODIUM

BUCKWHEAT BLINIS

Cut **4 ounces smoked salmon** into 1-inch pieces; set aside. Prepare Buckwheat Pancakes as directed but use only **1 teaspoon sugar** and drop batter by teaspoonfuls onto hot griddle. To serve, arrange 1 piece salmon on top of each blini and top each with ½ **teaspoon sour cream** (Cabot, Daisy, and Breakstone's brands are gluten-free) and **1 sprig dill**. Makes 30 blinis.

EACH BLINI: ABOUT 45 CALORIES | 2G PROTEIN | 4G CARBOHYDRATE | 3G TOTAL FAT (1G SATURATED) | 0G FIBER | 12MG CHOLESTEROL | 132MG SODIUM

BANANA BREAD

Studded with walnuts and bursting with banana flavor, this bread is so moist, you'd never guess it's gluten-free.

ACTIVE TIME: 25 MINUTES · **TOTAL TIME:** 1 HOUR 25 MINUTES
MAKES: 1 LARGE LOAF (16 SLICES)

1¾ CUPS ALL-PURPOSE FLOUR BLEND (PAGE 25)

1½ TEASPOONS BAKING POWDER

¾ TEASPOON BAKING SODA

½ TEASPOON XANTHAN GUM (SEE TIP)

¼ TEASPOON SALT

½ CUP BUTTER (1 STICK), SOFTENED

¾ CUP PACKED LIGHT BROWN SUGAR

2 LARGE EGGS

1 TEASPOON VANILLA EXTRACT (McCORMICK, SPICE ISLANDS, AND DURKEE BRANDS ARE GLUTEN-FREE)

1½ CUPS MASHED RIPE BANANAS (3 TO 4 LARGE)

½ CUP WALNUTS, CHOPPED

1 Preheat oven to 350°F. Grease 9" by 5" metal loaf pan. In medium bowl, whisk together flour blend, baking powder and soda, xanthan gum, and salt.
2 In large bowl, with mixer on medium speed, beat butter and brown sugar until light and creamy. Beat in eggs, one at a time. Beat in vanilla. Reduce speed to low; beat in flour mixture alternately with bananas, beginning and ending with flour mixture, scraping bowl occasionally. Stir in walnuts. Scrape batter into prepared pan.
3 Bake 50 to 60 minutes or until toothpick inserted in center of loaf comes out clean. Cool in pan on wire rack 10 minutes. Remove from pan and cool completely on wire rack.

TIP Despite its alien-sounding name, xanthan gum is a natural sugar derived from corn. This 100-percent gluten-free thickener is available at most health-food stores.

EACH SLICE: ABOUT 195 CALORIES | 2G PROTEIN | 28G CARBOHYDRATE | 9G TOTAL FAT (4G SATURATED | 2G FIBER | 38MG CHOLESTEROL | 210MG SODIUM

MORNING GLORY MUFFINS

Here is the ultimate breakfast muffin: a carrot cake–like batter dressed up with pecans, dried fruit, and a shredded Granny Smith apple to add a little tartness.

ACTIVE TIME: 20 MINUTES · **TOTAL TIME:** 45 MINUTES

MAKES: 12 MUFFINS

1½ CUPS ALL-PURPOSE FLOUR BLEND (PAGE 25)

1½ TEASPOONS GROUND CINNAMON

1 TEASPOON BAKING POWDER

1 TEASPOON BAKING SODA

1 TEASPOON XANTHAN GUM (SEE TIP, PAGE 39)

½ TEASPOON SALT

⅓ CUP PACKED BROWN SUGAR

⅓ CUP GRANULATED SUGAR

2 LARGE EGGS

⅓ CUP CANOLA OIL

1 CUP PACKAGED SHREDDED CARROT

1 GRANNY SMITH APPLE, PEELED, CORED, AND SHREDDED

½ CUP PECANS, CHOPPED

½ CUP DRIED FRUIT BITS OR GOLDEN RAISINS

1 Preheat oven to 375°F. Line 12-cup muffin pan with paper liners.

2 In medium bowl, combine flour blend, cinnamon, baking powder, baking soda, xanthan gum, and salt. In large bowl, stir together brown sugar, granulated sugar, eggs, and oil. Add flour mixture and stir until blended. Stir in carrot, apple, pecans, and dried fruit.

3 Spoon batter into muffin-pan cups. Bake 20 to 27 minutes or until toothpick inserted in center of muffins comes out clean. Remove to wire rack to cool.

EACH SERVING: ABOUT 225 CALORIES | 3G PROTEIN | 33G CARBOHYDRATE | 10G TOTAL FAT (1G SATURATED) | 2G FIBER | 31MG CHOLESTEROL | 268MG SODIUM 🍱

SANDWICHES, WRAPS & DIPS

In some cultures, lunch is the main meal, savored and followed by a siesta. In the United States, it tends to be grab-and-go—and your boss might nix the nap. But that doesn't mean lunch can't be a flavorful fix.

Fortunately, these recipes deliver protein for a midday boost of slow-burning energy along with faster-acting carbohydrates. And many of your options, sandwiches, wraps, salads, and more, can be packed in insulated containers so you can whip them out when your busy schedule allows. Among the wraps, you'll find a variety of creative, bread-free offerings like Homemade Sushi and Mango Chicken Lettuce Cups.

For recipes that call for the familiar, hearty presence of bread, you can choose to buy gluten-free products (see "Commercial Gluten-Free Breads," page 45) or make your own with our Homemade Sandwich Bread recipe, which not only provides everyday lunch foundations but the basis for bread crumbs that you can use in casseroles and other dishes. There are options for vegetarians and vegans, such as Rice and Bean Burgers, along with recipes with gluten-free, protein-packed chicken, salmon, and tuna. While you'll find gluten-free takes on favorites such as chicken salad, you'll also find offerings like Lemon-Cilantro Eggplant Dip, served with gluten-free pita wedges, that make fresh garden ingredients the main midday meal attraction.

Curried Chicken Pitas (page 48)

RICE AND BEAN BURGERS

Forget the bun and enjoy these mini "burger" patties wrapped up in flavored tortilla with a refreshing tahini-lemon yogurt sauce.

TOTAL TIME: 20 MINUTES

MAKES: 4 MAIN-DISH SERVINGS

1 LEMON	½ TEASPOON FENNEL SEEDS
1 CONTAINER (6 OUNCES) PLAIN LOW-FAT YOGURT	NONSTICK COOKING SPRAY
4 TABLESPOONS WELL-STIRRED TAHINI (SESAME PASTE)	4 BURRITO-SIZE (10-INCH) GLUTEN-FREE SPINACH OR RED CHILE TORTILLAS, SUCH AS SANDWICH PETALS BRAND
¾ TEASPOON SALT	2 CARROTS, PEELED AND SHREDDED
1 PACKAGE (8 TO 9 OUNCES) PRECOOKED BROWN RICE	2 RIPE PLUM TOMATOES, THINLY SLICED
1 CAN (15 TO 19 OUNCES) GARBANZO BEANS	1 KIRBY (PICKLING) CUCUMBER, NOT PEELED, THINLY SLICED
1 GARLIC CLOVE, CRUSHED WITH GARLIC PRESS	

1 Prepare outdoor grill for direct grilling over medium heat.

2 Meanwhile, from lemon, grate 1½ teaspoons peel and squeeze 2 tablespoons juice. In small serving bowl, stir lemon juice, yogurt, 2 tablespoons tahini, and ½ teaspoon salt until blended. Set yogurt sauce aside. (Makes about ¾ cup.)

3 Prepare rice in microwave oven as label directs. Set aside.

4 Reserve ¼ cup liquid from beans. Rinse beans and drain well. In medium bowl, combine beans, lemon peel, garlic, fennel seeds, remaining ¼ teaspoon salt, remaining 2 tablespoons tahini, and reserved bean liquid. With potato masher, coarsely mash bean mixture until well blended but still lumpy. Add rice and continue to mash just until blended.

5 Shape bean mixture into eight 1-inch-thick burgers. Coat both sides of burgers with cooking spray. Place burgers on very hot grill rack. Cook until well browned on the outside, 10 to 12 minutes, turning burgers over once.

6 To serve, place 2 burgers in center of each tortilla; top with sauce, carrots, tomatoes, and cucumber. Fold opposite sides of each tortilla over filling, then fold ends over to form a package.

EACH SERVING: ABOUT 465 CALORIES | 17G PROTEIN | 70G CARBOHYDRATE | 13G TOTAL FAT (2G SATURATED) | 10G FIBER | 3MG CHOLESTEROL | 588MG SODIUM ♥ ☻

COMMERCIAL GLUTEN-FREE BREADS

You might prefer to make your own gluten-free breads, but if you don't have the time or inclination, you have options for buying gluten-free products. Ask friends and online communities for recommendations; check Web reviews and give items a try. Many products are offered by small companies that distribute nationally through health food stores and grocers or make their wares available online. Check out products from Udi's Gluten Free Foods (udisglutenfree.com), which carries everything from gluten-free hamburger and hotdog buns to bagels and English muffins, Rudi's (rudisglutenfree.com), and Sandwich Petals (sandwichpetals.com), which makes three flavorful varieties of flatbread that can be used as tortillas and work well for wraps. (By the way, don't assume that corn tortillas are gluten-free: They may still be produced using wheat, so check labels with care. Mission corn tortillas, which are made from 100-percent corn, are labeled "gluten-free" on the package.) GFL Foods (glutenfreepitas.com) makes gluten-free pita bread, including a whole-grain version.

LEMON-CILANTRO EGGPLANT DIP

The rich, smoky taste of the roasted eggplant coupled with the citrus punch of the lemon juice and cilantro makes for a satisfying dip for toasted pita wedges and veggies. Or, turn it into a sandwich: Spread it on two slices of our Homemade Sandwich Bread (page 49) and top with sliced cucumbers, tomatoes, and alfalfa sprouts.

ACTIVE TIME: 10 MINUTES · TOTAL TIME: 55 MINUTES PLUS CHILLING

MAKES: 2 CUPS

---

2   EGGPLANTS (1 POUND EACH), EACH HALVED LENGTHWISE

4   GARLIC CLOVES, NOT PEELED

3   TABLESPOONS TAHINI (SESAME PASTE)

3   TABLESPOONS FRESH LEMON JUICE

¾   TEASPOON SALT

¼   CUP LOOSELY PACKED FRESH CILANTRO OR MINT LEAVES, CHOPPED

TOASTED OR GRILLED GLUTEN-FREE PITA WEDGES, SUCH AS GFL FOODS BRAND

CARROT AND CUCUMBER STICKS AND RED OR YELLOW PEPPER SLICES

1   Preheat oven to 450°F. Line 15½" by 10½" jelly-roll pan with nonstick foil (or use regular foil and spray with nonstick cooking spray). Place eggplant halves, skin-side up, in foil-lined pan. Wrap garlic in foil and place in pan with eggplants. Roast until eggplants are very tender and skin is shriveled and browned, 45 to 50 minutes. Unwrap garlic. Cool eggplants and garlic until easy to handle.

2   When cool, scoop eggplant flesh into food processor with knife blade attached. Squeeze out garlic pulp from each clove and add to food processor with tahini, lemon juice, and salt; pulse to coarsely chop. Spoon dip into serving bowl; stir in cilantro. Cover and refrigerate at least 2 hours.

3   Serve dip with pita and vegetables.

EACH TABLESPOON: ABOUT 10 CALORIES | 0G PROTEIN | 2G CARBOHYDRATE | 0G TOTAL FAT 1G FIBER | 0MG CHOLESTEROL | 55MG SODIUM ☺ ♥ 🍽

CURRIED CHICKEN PITAS

This curry-spiced chicken salad packs extra sweet flavor with the addition of cantaloupe. Serve it on toasted pita or atop peppery watercress or crisp romaine lettuce for a light and casual summer meal. For photo, see page 42.

TOTAL TIME: 20 MINUTES

MAKES: 4 SANDWICHES

¼ CUP PACKED FRESH CILANTRO LEAVES, FINELY CHOPPED

¼ CUP REDUCED-FAT SOUR CREAM (CABOT, DAISY, AND BREAKSTONE'S BRANDS ARE GLUTEN-FREE)

2 TABLESPOONS LOW-FAT MAYONNAISE

1 TABLESPOON FRESH LIME JUICE

1 TEASPOON GRATED, PEELED FRESH GINGER

¼ TEASPOON CURRY POWDER

¼ TEASPOON GROUND CORIANDER

⅛ TEASPOON SALT

2 CUPS CHOPPED, COOKED CHICKEN BREAST MEAT

5 RADISHES, CUT INTO ¼-INCH-THICK HALF-MOONS

1½ CUPS (8 OUNCES) CHOPPED CANTALOUPE

¼ SMALL RED ONION, FINELY CHOPPED

3 TABLESPOONS ROASTED CASHEWS, CHOPPED

4 GLUTEN-FREE PITA BREADS, SUCH AS GFL FOODS BRAND, TOASTED, EACH CUT INTO QUARTERS

1　In small bowl, whisk cilantro, sour cream, mayonnaise, lime juice, ginger, curry powder, coriander, and salt until well blended. If making ahead, cover and refrigerate up to 1 day.

2　In bowl, combine chicken, radishes, cantaloupe, and onion. If making ahead, cover and refrigerate up to 1 day. To serve, toss chicken mixture with half of dressing. Sprinkle with cashews. Spoon on top of pita pieces and serve with remaining dressing alongside.

EACH SERVING: ABOUT 375 CALORIES | 24G PROTEIN | 47G CARBOHYDRATE | 10G TOTAL FAT (3G SATURATED) | 2G FIBER | 67MG CHOLESTEROL | 640MG SODIUM ♥ ☺ 🍴

HOMEMADE SANDWICH BREAD

Banish dry, crumbly (not to mention costly!) storebought gluten-free bread with this delicious loaf. Bake it in multiples; the loaves can be wrapped tightly and frozen for later use.

ACTIVE TIME: 25 MINUTES · **TOTAL TIME:** 1 HOUR 10 MINUTES PLUS RISING AND COOLING
MAKES: 1 LARGE LOAF (16 SLICES)

1½ CUPS WARM WATER (105°F TO 115°F)	4 TEASPOONS XANTHAN GUM (SEE TIP, PAGE 39)
1 PACKAGE ACTIVE DRY YEAST	
2 TABLESPOONS PACKED BROWN SUGAR	2 TEASPOONS BAKING POWDER
2 CUPS ALL-PURPOSE FLOUR BLEND (PAGE 25)	1 TEASPOON SALT
1 CUP BROWN RICE FLOUR	2 LARGE EGGS AT ROOM TEMPERATURE
½ CUP MILLET FLOUR	4 TABLESPOONS BUTTER, MELTED
¼ CUP INSTANT NONFAT DRY MILK POWDER	1 TEASPOON APPLE CIDER VINEGAR

1   In small bowl, combine ¼ cup warm water, yeast, and 1 teaspoon brown sugar; stir and let stand 5 minutes, or until foamy.

2   In medium bowl, whisk remaining sugar, flour blend, brown rice flour, millet flour, milk powder, xanthan gum, baking powder, and salt.

3   In bowl of stand mixer fitted with paddle attachment (not dough hook), combine yeast mixture, remaining 1¼ cups warm water, eggs, butter, and vinegar. Beat on low speed until blended. Add flour mixture and beat on low speed until combined. Increase speed to medium and beat for 4 minutes, scraping sides of bowl occasionally.

4   Spray 9" by 5" metal loaf pan with cooking spray. Scrape batter into prepared pan and spread to fill pan, mounding batter slightly in center. Cover pan loosely with greased plastic wrap. Let sit in warm place until batter rises ½ inch above pan sides, 1 to 2 hours.

5   Preheat oven to 375°F. Bake 45 to 55 minutes or until loaf is well browned and instant-read thermometer registers 210°F when inserted in center of loaf, loosely tenting bread with foil if surface browns too much. Remove from pan and let cool completely on wire rack.

EACH SLICE: ABOUT 155 CALORIES | 3G PROTEIN | 27G CARBOHYDRATE | 7G TOTAL FAT (3G SATURATED) | 2G FIBER | 29MG CHOLESTEROL | 257MG SODIUM

OPEN-FACED SMOKED SALMON SANDWICHES

Turn a brunch treat into an elegant luncheon, swapping the gluten-loaded bagel for the chewy goodness of a gluten-free whole-grain bread.

TOTAL TIME: 20 MINUTES

MAKES: 4 SANDWICHES

---

1   LEMON

⅓   CUP (3 OUNCES) LIGHT CREAM CHEESE (PHILADELPHIA BRAND IS GLUTEN-FREE), SOFTENED

1   STALK CELERY, FINELY CHOPPED

½   CARROT, PEELED AND FINELY SHREDDED

2   TABLESPOONS DRAINED CAPERS

2   TABLESPOONS CHOPPED GREEN ONIONS

2   TEASPOONS CHOPPED FRESH DILL PLUS DILL SPRIGS FOR GARNISH

4   THIN SLICES (4 OUNCES) GLUTEN-FREE WHOLE-GRAIN BREAD OR HOMEMADE SANDWICH BREAD (PAGE 49)

1   PACKAGE (4 OUNCES) SLICED SMOKED SALMON

1   From lemon, grate 1 teaspoon peel and squeeze 1 tablespoon juice. In medium bowl, combine lemon peel and juice, cream cheese, celery, carrot, capers, green onions, and chopped dill. Stir to blend.

2   Spread cream cheese mixture on one side of each bread slice; top with smoked salmon. Cut each sandwich into quarters; garnish with dill sprigs to serve.

EACH SERVING: ABOUT 185 CALORIES | 10G PROTEIN | 21G CARBOHYDRATE | 7G TOTAL FAT (4G SATURATED) | 2G FIBER | 37MG CHOLESTEROL | 640MG SODIUM ☻ ☺

HEALTHY MAKEOVER TUNA SALAD

This deli and diner staple may be tasty and convenient, but it's not always the healthiest meal choice. Our makeover pairs down the fat, thanks to a mix of low-fat mayo and nonfat yogurt. Plus, veggies add flavor, crunch, fiber, and vitamins. Serve on our Homemade Sandwich Bread or over mixed greens.

TOTAL TIME: 15 MINUTES

MAKES: 2½ CUPS OR 4 SERVINGS

---

2 CANS (5 OUNCES EACH) CHUNK LIGHT TUNA IN WATER, DRAINED

2 STALKS CELERY, CHOPPED

1 CARROT, PEELED AND SHREDDED (½ CUP)

½ MEDIUM RED PEPPER (4 TO 6 OUNCES), CHOPPED

¼ CUP REDUCED-FAT MAYONNAISE (HELLMAN'S LITE MAYONNAISE IS GLUTEN-FREE)

3 TABLESPOONS NONFAT PLAIN YOGURT

1 TABLESPOON FRESH LEMON JUICE

¼ TEASPOON GROUND BLACK PEPPER

8 SLICES HOMEMADE SANDWICH BREAD (PAGE 49; OPTIONAL)

In a medium bowl, combine tuna, celery, carrot, red pepper, mayonnaise, yogurt, lemon juice, and pepper. Serve on bread if desired.

EACH SERVING: ABOUT 135 CALORIES | 16G PROTEIN | 6 CARBOHYDRATE | 6G TOTAL FAT (1G SATURATED) | 1G FIBER | 22MG CHOLESTEROL | 340MG SODIUM ♥ ☺ ♥

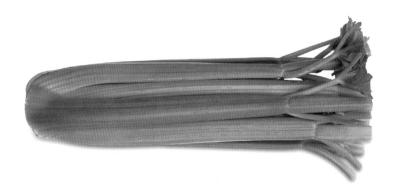

ROAST BEEF WALDORF CLUB SANDWICHES

Here's a Dagwood sandwich for the gluten-free gang. Horseradish dressing and a crunchy celery-and-apple mixture make rare roast beef taste even better. Soaking the onions in ice water crisps them and tames their bite.

TOTAL TIME: 20 MINUTES PLUS STANDING

MAKES: 4 SANDWICHES

---

4   VERY THIN SLICES RED ONION

½   GOLDEN DELICIOUS APPLE, PEELED AND FINELY CHOPPED (½ CUP)

2   STALKS CELERY, FINELY CHOPPED

4   TABLESPOONS REDUCED-FAT MAYONNAISE (HELLMAN'S LITE MAYONNAISE IS GLUTEN-FREE)

2   TABLESPOONS SOUR CREAM (CABOT, DAISY, AND BREAKSTONE'S BRANDS ARE GLUTEN-FREE)

½   TEASPOON FRESH LEMON JUICE

1   TABLESPOON BOTTLED WHITE HORSERADISH

12 THIN SLICES HOMEMADE SANDWICH BREAD (PAGE 49), LIGHTLY TOASTED, IF DESIRED

8   OUNCES THINLY SLICED RARE ROAST BEEF

1   BUNCH WATERCRESS (4 OUNCES), TOUGH STEMS TRIMMED

1   In small bowl, combine onion with enough ice water to cover; let stand 15 minutes. Drain.

2   In separate small bowl, combine apple, celery, 2 tablespoons mayonnaise, 1 tablespoon sour cream, and lemon juice until well blended. In cup, combine remaining 2 tablespoons mayonnaise, remaining 1 tablespoon sour cream, and horseradish until blended.

3   Spread horseradish mixture evenly on 4 bread slices. Layer roast beef, onion, and watercress on top. Spread celery mixture evenly on 4 bread slices and place, celery mixture up, over roast beef. Top with remaining bread slices. To serve, cut sandwiches in half.

EACH ½ SANDWICH: ABOUT 370 CALORIES | 12G PROTEIN | 58G CARBOHYDRATE 10G TOTAL FAT (5G SATURATED) | 5G FIBER | 76MG CHOLESTEROL | 842MG SODIUM ♥ ☺ ❦

MANGO CHICKEN LETTUCE CUPS

Skip the bread and wrap these speedy, no-cook chicken wraps in crisp lettuce leaves instead. Mango, fresh mint, and jicama add Latin-American zing.

TOTAL TIME: 20 MINUTES

MAKES: 4 MAIN-DISH SERVINGS

1   LARGE RIPE MANGO, PEELED AND CHOPPED

1   CUP FINELY CHOPPED JICAMA

½   CUP PACKED FRESH MINT LEAVES, FINELY CHOPPED

¼   CUP FRESH LIME JUICE

2   TABLESPOONS EXTRA-VIRGIN OLIVE OIL

½   TEASPOON ASIAN CHILI SAUCE (SRIRACHA), PLUS MORE TO TASTE

¼   TEASPOON SALT

3   CUPS COARSELY SHREDDED CHICKEN MEAT (FROM ½ ROTISSERIE CHICKEN)

12 BOSTON LETTUCE LEAVES

1   In large bowl, combine mango, jicama, mint, lime juice, oil, chili sauce, and salt. Toss to combine. If making ahead, cover bowl and refrigerate mixture up to overnight.

2   To serve, add chicken to mango mixture; toss to combine. Place ⅓ cup chicken mixture in each lettuce leaf.

EACH SERVING: ABOUT 325 CALORIES | 32G PROTEIN | 17G CARBOHYDRATE | 15G TOTAL FAT (3G SATURATED) | 4G FIBER | 94MG CHOLESTEROL | 400MG SODIUM ♥ ☺ ♥ ▬

HOMEMADE SUSHI

Sushi is the perfect gluten-free wrap. The fillings can be as varied as your tastes dicate (just steer clear of the imitation crab legs!), and the rolls can be made up to six hours ahead and refrigerated until you're ready to serve. Don't forget to provide your guests with plenty of pickled ginger, tamari, and wasabi on the side.

ACTIVE TIME: 1 HOUR 30 MINUTES · TOTAL TIME: 2 HOURS PLUS CHILLING
MAKES: 100 PIECES

FILLINGS

6 OUNCES COOKED SHELLED AND DEVEINED SHRIMP, THINLY SLICED LENGTHWISE

6 OUNCES THINLY SLICED SMOKED SALMON

1 RIPE AVOCADO

1 CARROT, PEELED AND CUT CROSSWISE IN HALF, THEN LENGTHWISE INTO PENCIL-THIN STICKS

1 SMALL CUCUMBER, CUT LENGTHWISE INTO 2" BY ¼" MATCHSTICK STRIPS

GARNISHES

BLACK SESAME SEEDS

WHITE SESAME SEEDS, TOASTED

MINCED FRESH CHIVES

ACCOMPANIMENTS

PICKLED GINGER

REDUCE-SODIUM TAMARI, SUCH AS SAN-J BRAND

WASABI (JAPANESE HORSERADISH)

SUSHI RICE AND WRAPPING

2½ CUPS WATER

2 CUPS JAPANESE SHORT-GRAIN RICE

2 TABLESPOONS SUGAR

1 TEASPOON SALT

½ CUP SEASONED RICE VINEGAR

1 PACKAGE (TEN 8" BY 7" SHEETS) ROASTED SEAWEED FOR SUSHI (NORI)

1 Assemble fillings: Place each filling in a small bowl. Cover bowls with plastic wrap and place in 15½" by 10½" jelly-roll pan for easy handling. Refrigerate fillings until ready to use.

2 Assemble garnishes and accompaniments: Place each garnish in a small bowl. Place each accompaniment in a small serving dish; cover. If not serving right away, refrigerate pickled ginger and wasabi.

3 Prepare sushi rice: In 3-quart saucepan, heat water, rice, sugar, and salt to boiling over high heat. Reduce heat to low; cover and simmer, without stirring or lifting lid, until rice is tender and liquid has been absorbed (rice will be sticky), about 25 minutes. Remove saucepan from heat; stir in vinegar. Cover and keep warm.

4 Make sushi rolls: Place sushi mat or 12-inch-long piece of plastic wrap on work surface. Place small bowl of water within reach of work area; it's easiest to handle sticky sushi rice with damp hands. (To make inside-out rolls, see Tip.)

5 Place 1 nori sheet, shiny (smooth) side down, with a short side facing you, on plastic wrap; top with generous ½ cup rice. With small metal spatula and damp hands, spread and pat rice into even layer over nori, leaving ¼-inch border all around sheet.

6 On top of rice, starting about 2 inches away from side facing you, arrange desired filling crosswise in 1½-inch-wide strip.

7 Using end of plastic wrap closest to you, lift edge of sushi, then firmly roll, jelly-roll fashion, away from you. Seal end of nori with water-dampened finger. Place sushi roll on tray or platter.

8 Repeat steps 5 through 7 to make 10 sushi rolls in all, changing plastic wrap when necessary. Cover and refrigerate sushi rolls 30 minutes or up to 6 hours.

9 To serve, with serrated knife, slice off and discard ends from each roll for a tidier presentation, if desired. Slice each roll crosswise into ten ½-inch-thick slices. Arrange sliced rolls on platter. Add garnishes as desired. Serve with accompaniments.

TIP To make an inside-out sushi roll, turn the rice-covered sheet of nori over at the end of step 5. Follow all other steps as indicated. During step 7 coat the outside of the roll with one of the garnishes.

EACH PIECE: ABOUT 25 CALORIES | 1G PROTEIN | 4G CARBOHYDRATE | 0G TOTAL FAT (0G SATURATED FAT) | 0G FIBER | 3MG CHOLESTEROL | 70MG SODIUM ☺ ♥

SALADS & SIDES

Our so-called side dishes might actually become the stars of the meal with their constellations of tantalizing, often colorful ingredients. Beyond their delicious taste and appealing presentation, these vegetable- and grain-based recipes provide a number of dietary elements that are especially important to people on a gluten-free diet, beginning with the ample fiber found in super grains like quinoa, the foundation for our Warm Quinoa Salad with Toasted Almonds and Warm Quinoa and Broccoli Salad, which is paired with a carrot-ginger dressing. Other fiber-filled offerings include Lentil Salad with Shrimp, Apples, and Mint—which provides fiber both in its lentil base and the crisp fruit—and a number of dishes that feature brown or wild rice.

The vegetables and beans that naturally play a defining role in our salads likewise provide essential nutrients, including ample amounts of protein (in beans) and antioxidant vitamins. But not everything is greens and beans: Our Asian Chicken Salad provides a zesty lime- and cilantro-seasoned option made from shredded, skinless rotisserie chicken meat with a crisp, colorful boost from shredded Napa cabbage and carrots. Whether you like your salads hot or cold, we've got options for every taste and every season.

Salad Niçoise (page 61)

ASIAN CHICKEN SALAD

Rotisserie chicken and thinly sliced Napa cabbage and carrots top naturally gluten-free vermicelli rice noodles. Fish sauce, lime juice, cilantro, and peanuts give this salad its Thai-inspired flavor.

ACTIVE TIME: 20 MINUTES · **TOTAL TIME:** 25 MINUTES

MAKES: 4 MAIN-DISH SERVINGS

6 CUPS WATER	4 CUPS THINLY SLICED NAPA CABBAGE (CHINESE CABBAGE; 1 SMALL HEAD)
4½ OUNCES VERMICELLI RICE NOODLES	2 CUPS PACKAGED SHREDDED CARROTS
¼ CUP LOWER-SODIUM ASIAN FISH SAUCE (A TASTE OF THAI AND CHUN'S BRAND MAKE GLUTEN-FREE VERSIONS)	½ CUP LOOSELY PACKED FRESH MINT LEAVES
3 TABLESPOONS FRESH LIME JUICE	½ CUP LOOSELY PACKED FRESH CILANTRO LEAVES
2 TABLESPOONS PACKED LIGHT BROWN SUGAR	½ CUP UNSALTED ROASTED PEANUTS, CHOPPED
¼ TEASPOON CRUSHED RED PEPPER	
2 CUPS SHREDDED, SKINLESS ROTISSERIE CHICKEN MEAT (10 OUNCES)	

1 In 8-cup glass measuring cup, microwave water on High 10 minutes. Add rice noodles; cook 1 to 2 minutes on High or until tender. Drain.

2 Meanwhile, in large bowl, combine fish sauce, lime juice, brown sugar, and crushed red pepper. Add chicken, cabbage, carrots, mint, and cilantro; toss to coat.

3 Divide noodles among four large dinner plates; top with chicken mixture. Sprinkle with peanuts to serve.

EACH SERVING: ABOUT 350 CALORIES | 27G PROTEIN | 30G CARBOHYDRATE | 15G TOTAL FAT (3G SATURATED) | 7G FIBER | 63MG CHOLESTEROL | 990MG SODIUM ♥ ☺ ✿

SALAD NIÇOISE

This classic French composed salad is the perfect entrée for a ladies' lunch or light dinner. For photo, see page 58.

ACTIVE TIME: 30 MINUTES · TOTAL TIME: 1 HOUR 5 MINUTES
MAKES: 6 MAIN-DISH SERVINGS

⅓ CUP LOOSELY PACKED FRESH PARSLEY LEAVES, CHOPPED

¼ CUP RED WINE VINEGAR

3 TABLESPOONS OLIVE OIL

1 TEASPOON DIJON MUSTARD (GREY POUPON AND MAILLE BRANDS ARE GLUTEN-FREE)

¼ TEASPOON SALT

¼ TEASPOON GROUND BLACK PEPPER

1 POUND SMALL RED POTATOES

6 LARGE EGGS

½ POUND GREEN BEANS, TRIMMED AND EACH CUT CROSSWISE IN HALF

1 BAG (5 OUNCES) MIXED BABY GREENS (8 CUPS LOOSELY PACKED)

½ ENGLISH (SEEDLESS) CUCUMBER, THINLY SLICED

1 CAN (12 OUNCES) SOLID WHITE TUNA IN WATER, DRAINED

3 MEDIUM TOMATOES, CUT INTO WEDGES

½ CUP NIÇOISE OLIVES (3 OUNCES)

1 Into small bowl, measure parsley, vinegar, oil, mustard, salt, and pepper. Mix vinaigrette with wire whisk or fork until blended; set aside.

2 In 3-quart saucepan, place unpeeled potatoes and enough *water* to cover; heat to boiling over high heat. Reduce heat to low; simmer 10 to 12 minutes or until potatoes are fork-tender.

3 Meanwhile, in 2-quart saucepan, place eggs and enough *cold water* to cover by 1 inch; heat to boiling over high heat. Remove saucepan from heat and cover tightly; let stand 15 minutes. Pour off hot water; run cold water over eggs to cool. Remove shells and cut each egg into wedges.

4 When potatoes are done, with slotted spoon, transfer to colander to drain. To same water in saucepan, add beans; heat to boiling over high heat. Reduce heat to low; simmer 5 to 10 minutes or until tender-crisp. Drain beans; rinse with cold running water to stop cooking; drain again.

5 In large bowl, toss greens with half of vinaigrette. Place greens on large platter. Cut each potato in half or quarters if large; transfer to platter with greens. Arrange beans, eggs, cucumber, tuna, tomatoes, and olives in separate piles on same platter; drizzle with remaining vinaigrette.

EACH SERVING: ABOUT 315 CALORIES | 22G PROTEIN | 24G CARBOHYDRATE | 15G TOTAL FAT (3G SATURATED) | 4G FIBER | 233MG CHOLESTEROL | 515MG SODIUM ☺

SIX-BEAN SALAD WITH TOMATO VINAIGRETTE

This salad is a tasty powerhouse of protein, iron, and bone-building vitamin K. The tomato dressing contributes a zesty finish.

ACTIVE TIME: 20 MINUTES · TOTAL TIME: 26 MINUTES PLUS CHILLING
MAKES: 18 SIDE-DISH SERVINGS

1 TEASPOON SALT

8 OUNCES GREEN BEANS, TRIMMED AND CUT INTO 1-INCH PIECES

8 OUNCES WAX BEANS, TRIMMED AND CUT INTO 1-INCH PIECES

1 CAN (15 TO 19 OUNCES) GARBANZO BEANS

1 CAN (15 TO 19 OUNCES) BLACK BEANS OR BLACK SOYBEANS

1 CAN (15 TO 19 OUNCES) RED KIDNEY BEANS

1½ CUPS (HALF 16-OUNCE BAG) FROZEN SHELLED EDAMAME (GREEN SOYBEANS), THAWED

TOMATO VINAIGRETTE

1 SMALL RIPE TOMATO (4 OUNCES), COARSELY CHOPPED

1 SMALL SHALLOT, COARSELY CHOPPED

¼ CUP OLIVE OIL

2 TABLESPOONS RED WINE VINEGAR

1 TABLESPOON DIJON MUSTARD (GREY POUPON AND MAILLE BRANDS ARE GLUTEN-FREE)

½ TEASPOON SALT

¼ TEASPOON GROUND BLACK PEPPER

1 In 12-inch skillet, heat *1 inch water* with salt to boiling over high heat. Add green and wax beans; return water to a boil. Reduce heat to low; simmer until beans are tender-crisp, 6 to 8 minutes. Drain beans. Rinse with cold running water to stop cooking; drain again. Transfer beans to large serving bowl.

2 While green and wax beans are cooking, rinse and drain garbanzo, black, and kidney beans. Add canned beans and edamame to bowl with green and wax beans.

3 Prepare Tomato Vinaigrette: In blender, combine tomato, shallot, oil, vinegar, mustard, salt, and pepper. Blend until smooth.

4 Add vinaigrette to beans in bowl. Toss until beans are evenly coated with vinaigrette. Cover and refrigerate at least 1 hour to blend flavors or up to 8 hours.

EACH SERVING: ABOUT 130 CALORIES | 7G PROTEIN | 17G CARBOHYDRATE | 4G TOTAL FAT (0G SATURATED) | 6G FIBER | 0MG CHOLESTEROL | 230MG SODIUM ☺ ♥ ❂ 🍴

LENTIL SALAD WITH SHRIMP, APPLES, AND MINT

This heart-healthy salad is chock-full of fiber, thanks to crisp Golden Delicious apples and a lentil base.

ACTIVE TIME: 15 MINUTES · TOTAL TIME: 30 MINUTES
MAKES: 4 MAIN-DISH SERVINGS

3 TABLESPOONS OLIVE OIL

3 TABLESPOONS CIDER VINEGAR

1½ TEASPOONS SALT

¼ TEASPOON GROUND BLACK PEPPER

1 POUND FRESH OR FROZEN (THAWED) SHELLED AND DEVEINED MEDIUM SHRIMP

1 CUP LENTILS

6 CUPS WATER

1 SMALL ONION (4 TO 6 OUNCES), CHOPPED

½ CUP LOOSELY PACKED FRESH MINT LEAVES, CHOPPED

1 GOLDEN DELICIOUS APPLE, NOT PEELED, CORED, AND CUT INTO ½-INCH CHUNKS

1 STALK CELERY, THINLY SLICED

1 In small bowl, whisk oil, vinegar, salt, and pepper. Spoon 2 tablespoons dressing into medium bowl. Add shrimp; toss to coat.

2 In colander, rinse lentils with cold water and discard any stones or shriveled lentils. In 4-quart saucepan, combine lentils, water, onion, and 2 tablespoons mint; heat to boiling over high heat. Reduce heat to low; cover and simmer 8 to 10 minutes or until lentils are tender but still hold shape. Drain well.

3 Meanwhile, heat 12-inch skillet over medium-high heat until hot. Add shrimp with any dressing and cook 4 to 5 minutes or until shrimp turn opaque. Remove from heat; stir in 1 tablespoon mint.

4 Stir shrimp, apple, celery, remaining mint, and remaining dressing into lentils. Serve warm.

EACH SERVING: ABOUT 410 CALORIES | 37G PROTEIN | 37G CARBOHYDRATE | 13G TOTAL FAT (2G SATURATED) | 17G FIBER | 172MG CHOLESTEROL | 475MG SODIUM ✓ ☺ ❀

WARM QUINOA AND BROCCOLI SALAD

Quinoa, an ancient grain that's naturally gluten-free, ups the protein and fiber quotient of this Asian-inspired salad, which pairs perfectly with marinated grilled beef. A gingery carrot dressing adds zip.

ACTIVE TIME: 15 MINUTES · TOTAL TIME: 35 MINUTES
MAKES: 6 SIDE-DISH SERVINGS

1½ CUPS QUINOA, THOROUGHLY RINSED

3¼ CUPS PLUS 3 TABLESPOONS WATER

¾ TEASPOON SALT

1 BAG (10 OUNCES) BROCCOLI FLOWERETS

⅔ CUP CHOPPED, PEELED CARROT (ABOUT 1 LARGE)

3 TABLESPOONS FINELY CHOPPED, PEELED FRESH GINGER

3 TABLESPOONS VEGETABLE OIL

2 TABLESPOONS SEASONED RICE VINEGAR

2 TEASPOONS REDUCED-SODIUM TAMARI SAUCE, SUCH AS SAN-J BRAND

2 TEASPOONS ASIAN SESAME OIL

1   In 3-quart saucepan, combine quinoa, 3 cups water, and ½ teaspoon salt; heat to boiling over high heat. Reduce heat to low; cover and simmer until water is absorbed, about 20 minutes. Transfer quinoa to large bowl.

2   Meanwhile, place broccoli and ¼ cup water in microwave-safe medium bowl; cover and cook in microwave on High 4 to 5 minutes or until tender-crisp. Drain; add to quinoa in bowl.

3   In blender, combine carrot, ginger, vegetable oil, vinegar, tamari, sesame oil, remaining 3 tablespoons water, and remaining ¼ teaspoon salt; blend until pureed. Add to quinoa and broccoli and toss to combine. Serve salad warm or at room temperature.

EACH SERVING: ABOUT 265 CALORIES | 7G PROTEIN | 36G CARBOHYDRATE | 11G TOTAL FAT (1G SATURATED) | 4G FIBER | 0MG CHOLESTEROL | 605MG SODIUM

GLUTEN-FREE GRAINS

Because many grains are off-limits for people with celiac disease or gluten sensitivity, gluten-free grains are bedrock items in a gluten-free diet. They can sometimes be purchased in bulk at health food stores, though you should be wary of cross-contamination (for more information on cross-contamination, see page 18). Among the primary grains used in gluten-free cooking:

Amaranth: Once a key grain in Aztec culture, it's loaded with fiber and protein and has a peppery flavor.

Buckwheat: Not actually wheat, it's a plant whose seed contains a kernel called a groat that you can boil to eat as a hot cereal, roast for a side dish, or mill into a flour that can be used for pancakes. Buckwheat flour is also used to make some Asian noodles. Be cautious when buying buckwheat and check labels when buying noodles made with buckwheat flour: Buckwheat is sometimes mixed with regular wheat.

Corn: Perhaps the most familiar grain to Americans, cornmeal and products like corn flour and cornstarch can often be substituted for wheat flour. Some cornstarch may contain wheat; see Tip, page 34.

Millet: Among the most ancient of grains, grown worldwide, millet is abundant in B vitamins and fiber, and contains moderate amounts of protein. It's best toasted, then boiled in water like rice.

Quinoa: Cultivated for thousands of years in South America, it's packed with protein and nutrients including B vitamins, iron, calcium, and fiber. Thorough rinsing removes the bitter coating.

Rice: It's familiar and versatile; opt for brown rice over white varieties. Because it's been stripped of its bran and germ, white rice (including the flavorful basmati) has only a shadow of the nutritive value of brown rice, even though it's often enriched. Brown rice generally takes longer to cook than white, but it's worth the wait, as different varieties can introduce new flavors and textures.

Teff: Though relatively new to Americans, it's a staple in parts of Africa. Featuring a sweet, nutty flavor, it's richer in calcium and iron than most other grains and also provides protein and fiber.

Wild rice: A native North American grass (not technically a rice), it provides zinc, magnesium, and folate and makes an excellent side dish. Because of its relatively high cost and assertive, earthy flavor, it is often used in tandem with white or brown rice.

WARM QUINOA SALAD WITH TOASTED ALMONDS

Often called a supergrain because it contains all eight essential amino acids, quinoa is considered a complete protein. Toasting quinoa brings out its delicate nutty flavor and reduces its bitter aftertaste.

ACTIVE TIME: 5 MINUTES · TOTAL TIME: 30 MINUTES

MAKES: 5 SIDE-DISH SERVINGS

1½ CUPS QUINOA, THOROUGHLY RINSED

2½ CUPS PLUS 1 TABLESPOON WATER

½ TEASPOON SALT

2 TABLESPOONS REDUCED-SODIUM TAMARI, SUCH AS SAN-J BRAND

1 TABLESPOON RICE VINEGAR

1 TEASPOON ASIAN SESAME OIL

1 TEASPOON GRATED, PEELED FRESH GINGER

2 GREEN ONIONS, THINLY SLICED DIAGONALLY

¼ CUP SLICED NATURAL ALMONDS, TOASTED

1   In 12-inch dry skillet, toast quinoa over medium heat until fragrant and golden, about 5 minutes, stirring frequently.

2   Stir 2½ cups water and salt into toasted quinoa; heat to boiling over high heat. Reduce heat to low; cover and simmer until all water is absorbed, 15 to 17 minutes.

3   Meanwhile, in small bowl, stir together tamari, vinegar, oil, ginger, green onions, and remaining 1 tablespoon water.

4   Transfer quinoa to large serving bowl. Stir in tamari mixture until quinoa is evenly coated. Sprinkle with toasted almonds to serve.

EACH SERVING: ABOUT 305 CALORIES | 9G PROTEIN | 38G CARBOHYDRATE

7G TOTAL FAT (1G SATURATED) | 4G FIBER | 0MG CHOLESTEROL | 460MG SODIUM

WILD RICE PILAF WITH CRANBERRIES

A festive side dish for any occasion, this pistachio- and cranberry-studded rice pilaf recipe serves sixteen—an ample amount for a jolly-good holiday meal.

TOTAL TIME: 1 HOUR

MAKES: 16 SIDE-DISH SERVINGS

2   CUPS WILD RICE (12 OUNCES)

6   CUPS WATER

1½ CUPS DRIED CRANBERRIES OR DRIED TART CHERRIES

2   TABLESPOONS BUTTER

4   CARROTS, PEELED AND CHOPPED

2   LARGE STALKS CELERY, CHOPPED

1   LARGE ONION (12 OUNCES), CHOPPED

2   CUPS REGULAR LONG-GRAIN WHITE RICE

1   CAN (14 TO 14½ OUNCES) GLUTEN-FREE CHICKEN BROTH (1¾ CUP), SUCH AS SWANSON BRAND

1   TEASPOON SALT

½   TEASPOON GROUND BLACK PEPPER

½   CUP LOOSELY PACKED FRESH PARSLEY LEAVES, CHOPPED

4   OUNCES PISTACHIO NUTS, SHELLS REMOVED (½ CUP), TOASTED AND CHOPPED

1   In 4-quart saucepan, heat wild rice and 4 cups water to boiling over high heat. Reduce heat to low; cover and simmer 35 to 40 minutes or until wild rice is tender and grains begin to split. Stir in cranberries; cook 1 minute. Drain wild rice mixture; keep warm in covered saucepan until ready to use.

2   Meanwhile, in heavy 5-quart Dutch oven, melt butter over medium-high heat. Add carrots, celery, and onion; cook 13 to 15 minutes or until vegetables are tender and lightly browned, stirring occasionally. Transfer vegetables to medium bowl and set aside at room temperature until all rice is done.

3   In same Dutch oven, heat white rice, broth, and remaining 2 cups water to boiling over high heat. Reduce heat to low; cover pot and simmer 16 to 18 minutes or until rice is tender and all liquid is absorbed.

4   Into white rice in Dutch oven, stir wild-rice mixture, vegetable mixture, salt, and pepper; cook over medium-low heat until pilaf is heated through.

5   Just before serving, gently stir parsley and pistachio nuts into pilaf until evenly distributed. Transfer to large serving bowl.

EACH SERVING: ABOUT 245 CALORIES | 6G PROTEIN | 48G CARBOHYDRATE | 4G TOTAL FAT (1G SATURATED) | 4G FIBER | 0MG CHOLESTEROL | 245MG SODIUM

MILLET WITH CORN AND GREEN CHILES

Millet has a mild flavor that is greatly enhanced by pan-toasting it first. For an extra shot of flavor, serve this satisfying side topped with a dollop of your favorite salsa.

ACTIVE TIME: 25 MINUTES · TOTAL TIME: 50 MINUTES
MAKES: 8 SIDE-DISH SERVINGS

1   CUP MILLET

2   CUPS CORN KERNELS CUT FROM COBS (ABOUT 4 EARS), OR FROZEN CORN KERNELS

2   TEASPOONS VEGETABLE OIL

1   ONION, CHOPPED

1   GARLIC CLOVE, CRUSHED WITH GARLIC PRESS

1   TEASPOON GROUND CUMIN

3½ CUPS WATER

1   CAN (4½ OUNCES) DICED GREEN CHILES, DRAINED, SUCH AS CHI-CHI'S BRAND

½   TEASPOON SALT

¼   CUP LIGHTLY PACKED FRESH CILANTRO LEAVES, CHOPPED (OPTIONAL)

1 In large dry skillet, cook millet over medium heat until toasted, about 5 minutes, stirring frequently. Pour millet into bowl and set aside.

2 Add corn to dry skillet and cook over high heat until browned, about 5 minutes, stirring frequently. Transfer corn to plate.

3 In same skillet, heat oil over medium heat. Add onion; cook until softened, about 5 minutes. Stir in garlic and cumin and cook until fragrant, about 1 minute. Add water, green chiles, and salt and bring to a boil. Stir in millet. Reduce heat; cover and simmer until millet is tender and water is absorbed, 25 to 30 minutes.

4 Remove skillet from heat and stir in corn; cover and let stand 5 minutes to heat through. Stir in cilantro, if using.

EACH SERVING: ABOUT 150 CALORIES | 4G PROTEIN, 29G CARBOHYDRATE | 3G TOTAL FAT (0G SATURATED) | 4G FIBER | 0MG CHOLESTEROL | 200MG SODIUM ☺ ♥ ▤

ASPARAGUS GREMOLATA

For this fresh-as-spring side, blanched asparagus is blanketed with a lemony mixture of crisp crumbs and herbs. Panko are crisp, light Japanese bread crumbs. Le Garden brand makes gluten-free panko, including a whole-wheat version.

ACTIVE TIME: 20 MINUTES · TOTAL TIME: 30 MINUTES

MAKES: 6 SIDE-DISH SERVINGS

1¼ TEASPOONS SALT

2 POUNDS JUMBO ASPARAGUS, TRIMMED AND PEELED

1 GARLIC CLOVE, FINELY CHOPPED

1 TABLESPOON PLUS 1 TEASPOON EXTRA-VIRGIN OLIVE OIL

1 TEASPOON FRESHLY GRATED LEMON PEEL

¼ CUP GLUTEN-FREE PANKO, SUCH AS LE GARDEN BRAND

¼ CUP PACKED FRESH FLAT-LEAF PARSLEY LEAVES, FINELY CHOPPED

¼ TEASPOON GROUND BLACK PEPPER

1   Heat large covered saucepot of *water* to boiling over high heat. Fill large bowl with ice water.

2   Add 1 teaspoon salt, then asparagus, to boiling water. Cook uncovered 5 to 6 minutes or until asparagus is bright green and knife pierces stalks easily. With tongs, transfer directly to bowl of ice water. When asparagus is cool, drain well. Roll between paper towels to dry completely. The cooked asparagus can be refrigerated in an airtight container or resealable plastic bag up to overnight.

3   In 12-inch skillet, combine garlic, 1 tablespoon oil, and ½ teaspoon lemon peel. Cook over medium heat 2 minutes or until golden, stirring occasionally. Add panko and cook 1 to 2 minutes or until golden and toasted, stirring frequently. Transfer to small bowl; wipe out skillet.

4   In same skillet, combine asparagus, 1 *tablespoon water*, and remaining 1 teaspoon oil. Cook over medium heat 2 to 5 minutes or until heated through, turning frequently. Transfer to serving platter.

5   Stir parsley, remaining ½ teaspoon lemon peel, remaining ¼ teaspoon salt, and pepper into panko mixture. Spoon seasoned panko over asparagus.

EACH SERVING: ABOUT 60 CALORIES | 2G PROTEIN | 5G CARBOHYDRATE | 4G TOTAL FAT (0G SATURATED) | 2G FIBER | 3MG CHOLESTEROL | 157MG SODIUM ❤ ☺ ♥ 🍴

SKILLET CORN BREAD

This delicious homemade corn bread is baked in an oven-safe skillet—preferably one that's heavyweight, such as cast iron. Cornmeal is naturally gluten-free, but due to cross-contamination, many brands are not guaranteed gluten-free. See our suggestions below.

ACTIVE TIME: 10 MINUTES · TOTAL TIME: 35 MINUTES PLUS COOLING

MAKES: 8 SIDE-DISH SERVINGS

2   CUPS CORNMEAL (BOB'S RED MILL AND ARROWHEAD MILLS BRANDS ARE GUARANTEED GLUTEN-FREE)

¼   CUP SUGAR

2   TABLESPOONS GLUTEN-FREE CORNSTARCH

1   TABLESPOON BAKING POWDER

1   TEASPOON BAKING SODA

1   TEASPOON SALT

2   CUPS BUTTERMILK

2   LARGE EGGS

¼   CUP VEGETABLE OIL

1   Place 9-inch cast-iron skillet in oven, then preheat oven to 425°F.

2   In large bowl, combine cornmeal, sugar, cornstarch, baking powder, baking soda, and salt. In medium bowl, whisk buttermilk, eggs, and oil until blended; stir into cornmeal mixture just until batter is smooth.

3   Coat inside of preheated skillet with cooking spray. Pour batter into skillet. Bake 20 to 25 minutes or until toothpick inserted in center of corn bread comes out clean.

EACH SERVING: ABOUT 250 CALORIES | 6G PROTEIN | 36G CARBOHYDRATE | 10G TOTAL FAT (1G SATURATED) | 2G FIBER | 49MG CHOLESTEROL | 747MG SODIUM

SOUPS, STEWS & CHILIS

The embodiment of comfort food, a bowl of soup or stew brings to mind images of home and hearth that seem both up-to-date and timeless. In fact, with their bounty of fresh ingredients and simplicity of presentation, these dishes are thought to be as old as cooking itself; variations on the put-it-in-the-pot theme can be found in virtually every culture. You'll get a sense of that cultural variety from a number of the recipes here, including Vietnamese Rice Noodle Soup, Fish Stew, and Pork Posole.

But the variety isn't limited to origins or ethnicity. The gluten-free foundations of the recipes in this chapter range from dishes that will stuff your bowl with vegetables (naturally gluten-free) to combinations that include ingredients such as vermicelli rice noodles, hominy, meat, and even fruit. We haven't forgotten the comfort aspect, either: You'll find longtime favorites like Mushroom and Brown Rice Soup and Mixed Vegetable Minestrone. They pack ample portions of hearty vegetables such as onion and carrots, along with savory and satisfying extras such as bacon and tubetti pasta. You can also discover new flavor combinations in recipes like the Carrot and Apple Soup. One note: Canned broths may be a source of hidden gluten, so be sure to check labels (or use the gluten-free brands we've listed in the recipes). Pull up a chair—soup's on!

Mixed Vegetable Minestrone (page 81)

CHILLED CORN AND BACON SOUP

Light but lush—thickened with late-season corn rather than flour, low-fat milk, and a Yukon Gold potato—this refreshing farm-stand soup is summer's answer to cold-weather chowders.

ACTIVE TIME: 25 MINUTES · **TOTAL TIME:** 35 MINUTES PLUS CHILLING
MAKES: 4 MAIN-DISH SERVINGS

---

4   SLICES THICK-CUT BACON (SMITH'S, HORMEL, AND OSCAR MEYER OFFER GLUTEN-FREE OPTIONS; SEE TIP), CUT INTO ½-INCH PIECES

1   LARGE SHALLOT, FINELY CHOPPED

3   CUPS CORN KERNELS CUT FROM COBS (ABOUT 6 EARS)

1   LARGE YUKON GOLD POTATO (8 OUNCES), PEELED AND SHREDDED

⅛   TEASPOON SMOKED PAPRIKA PLUS ADDITIONAL FOR GARNISH

⅔   CUP WATER

4   CUPS LOW-FAT (1%) MILK

⅛   TEASPOON SALT

⅛   TEASPOON GROUND BLACK PEPPER

¼   CUP PACKED FRESH CILANTRO LEAVES

1   In 12-inch skillet, cook bacon over medium heat 6 to 8 minutes or until crisp and browned. With slotted spoon, transfer to paper towels to drain. If making ahead, cover and refrigerate up to overnight.

2   Drain and discard all but 1 tablespoon fat from skillet. Add shallot and cook over medium heat 2 minutes or until golden and tender, stirring occasionally. Add 2½ cups corn, potato, and paprika. Cook 2 minutes, stirring, then add water and cook 7 minutes or until liquid evaporates and vegetables are tender.

3   Remove skillet from heat and transfer corn mixture to blender. Add milk and salt and puree until mixture is very smooth. Cover and refrigerate until soup is cold, at least 3 hours and up to overnight.

4   To serve, divide among serving bowls. Top with bacon, pepper, cilantro, and remaining ½ cup corn. Garnish with paprika.

TIP Some bacons contain gluten; it is primarily used as a filler. Start with the brands we recommend above and read labels with care.

EACH SERVING: ABOUT 375 CALORIES | 17G PROTEIN | 54G CARBOHYDRATE | 12G TOTAL FAT (5G SATURATED) | 5G FIBER | 23MG CHOLESTEROL | 750MG SODIUM ☺ 🌱 🍴

TOMATO SOUP WITH TOFU-PARMESAN CROUTONS

This luscious tomato soup is garnished with a surprise: baked croutons made from Parmesan-encrusted tofu. Use a store-bought gluten-free bread—preferably whole-grain—or a day-old slice of our Homemade Sandwich Bread (page 49) to make the crumbs.

ACTIVE TIME: 15 MINUTES · **TOTAL TIME:** 40 MINUTES

MAKES: 4 FIRST-COURSE SERVINGS

1	TABLESPOON OLIVE OIL	½	TEASPOON SALT
1	CUP PACKAGED SHREDDED CARROTS	¼	TEASPOON GROUND BLACK PEPPER
1	SMALL ONION (4 TO 6 OUNCES), FINELY CHOPPED	1	PACKAGE (14 OUNCES) FIRM TOFU, DRAINED
2	GARLIC CLOVES, CRUSHED WITH GARLIC PRESS	1	SLICE GLUTEN-FREE WHOLE-GRAIN BREAD, COARSELY GRATED INTO CRUMBS
2	CANS (28 OUNCES EACH) WHOLE TOMATOES IN JUICE	½	CUP FRESHLY GRATED PARMESAN CHEESE
1	CUP WATER		

1 In 6-quart saucepot, heat oil over medium-high heat. Add carrots, onion, and garlic and cook, covered, 5 to 7 minutes or until vegetables begin to brown, stirring occasionally.

2 Stir in tomatoes with their juice, water, salt, and pepper, breaking up tomatoes with spoon; heat to boiling. Reduce heat to medium-low; partially cover and simmer 20 minutes.

3 Meanwhile, preheat broiler for making croutons. Cut tofu into 8 slices. Place slices between layers of paper towels and gently press to extract excess moisture. In bowl, combine bread crumbs and Parmesan. Spray cookie sheet with nonstick cooking spray. Arrange tofu on cookie sheet; sprinkle with crumb mixture. Place cookie sheet in broiler, 5 to 6 inches from source of heat, and broil tofu 5 to 8 minutes or until browned.

4 To serve, with potato masher, crush tomatoes in soup. Top each serving of soup with 2 croutons.

EACH SERVING: ABOUT 270 CALORIES | 16G PROTEIN | 31G CARBOHYDRATE | 12G TOTAL FAT (3G SATURATED) | 6G FIBER | 7MG CHOLESTEROL | 1,125MG SODIUM ☺ 🌱

MIXED VEGETABLE MINESTRONE

Tubetti pasta is available gluten-free, but you can also substitute larger gluten-free noodles broken into small pieces prior to cooking. For photo, see page 76.

ACTIVE TIME: 18 MINUTES · **TOTAL TIME:** 40 MINUTES

MAKES: 6 MAIN-DISH SERVINGS

- 2 TABLESPOONS OLIVE OIL
- 1 MEDIUM ONION (6 TO 8 OUNCES), FINELY CHOPPED
- 2 GARLIC CLOVES, CRUSHED WITH GARLIC PRESS
- ¾ TEASPOON SALT
- ¾ TEASPOON GROUND BLACK PEPPER
- 1 CAN (28 OUNCES) DICED TOMATOES
- 4 CUPS WATER
- 1 POUND CARROTS, PEELED AND CUT INTO ½-INCH PIECES
- 1 SMALL BUNCH (12 OUNCES) SWISS CHARD, STEMS DISCARDED, LEAVES THINLY SLICED (5½ CUPS)
- 8 OUNCES GREEN BEANS, TRIMMED AND CUT INTO 1-INCH PIECES
- 1½ CUPS FROZEN SHELLED EDAMAME (GREEN SOYBEANS)
- 1 CAN (15 OUNCES) LOW-SODIUM WHITE KIDNEY (CANNELLINI) BEANS, RINSED AND DRAINED
- 1 CUP GLUTEN-FREE TUBETTI OR OTHER SHORT PASTA, SUCH AS SAM MILLS OR LE VENEZIANE BRANDS
- ½ CUP PLUS 6 TABLESPOONS FRESHLY GRATED PARMESAN CHEESE

1 In 5- to 6-quart saucepot, heat 1 tablespoon oil over medium heat until hot. Stir in onion, garlic, ½ teaspoon salt, and ½ teaspoon pepper. Cover and cook 4 to 5 minutes or until tender. Add tomatoes and water. Heat to boiling over medium-high heat. Add carrots; cover and cook 10 minutes, stirring occasionally. Add chard and green beans; cook 6 minutes or until beans are just tender, stirring occasionally. Add edamame and white beans; cook 5 minutes or until edamame are just cooked through. (Can be prepared to this point up to 2 days ahead; transfer to airtight container and refrigerate. Reheat before continuing with recipe.)

2 Meanwhile, cook pasta as label directs. Drain well and stir into saucepot with soup. Stir in ½ cup Parmesan and remaining ¼ teaspoon each salt and pepper. Ladle into six soup bowls. Top each portion with 1 tablespoon Parmesan and ½ teaspoon oil.

EACH SERVING: ABOUT 575 CALORIES | 38G PROTEIN | 63G CARBOHYDRATE | 21G TOTAL FAT (3G SATURATED) | 17G FIBER | 7MG CHOLESTEROL | 775MG SODIUM ⚘ ▣

MUSHROOM AND BROWN RICE SOUP

Wholesome brown rice makes this soup hearty, while wild mushrooms add depth of flavor. A mixed green salad with an herb vinaigrette makes it a meal.

ACTIVE TIME: 25 MINUTES · **TOTAL TIME:** 30 MINUTES

MAKES: 8 CUPS OR 4 MAIN-DISH SERVINGS

1   TABLESPOON OLIVE OIL

1   MEDIUM ONION, FINELY CHOPPED

1   PACKAGE (10 OUNCES) SLICED WHITE MUSHROOMS

1   PACKAGE (4 OUNCES) SLICED ASSORTED WILD MUSHROOMS

1   CUP PACKAGED SHREDDED CARROTS

1   GARLIC CLOVE, CRUSHED WITH GARLIC PRESS

½   TEASPOON SALT

¼   TEASPOON DRIED THYME

⅛   TEASPOON GROUND BLACK PEPPER

1   CARTON (32 OUNCES) GLUTEN-FREE CHICKEN BROTH, SUCH AS PROGRESSO, IMAGINE, OR PACIFIC NATURAL FOODS BRANDS

¾   CUP INSTANT BROWN RICE

2   CUPS WATER

1   In 4-quart saucepan, heat oil over medium-high heat. Add onion and cook 5 minutes, stirring occasionally. Add white and wild mushrooms and carrots and cook until mushrooms are golden and tender, 8 to 10 minutes, stirring occasionally. Add garlic, salt, thyme, and pepper and cook 1 minute, stirring.

2   Add broth, rice, and water; cover and heat to boiling over high heat. Reduce heat to medium; cook soup, partially covered, until rice is tender, about 5 minutes.

EACH SERVING: ABOUT 155 CALORIES | 6G PROTEIN | 24G CARBOHYDRATE | 4G TOTAL FAT (1G SATURATED) | 3G FIBER | 0MG CHOLESTEROL | 856MG SODIUM ● ☺ 🛒

CARROT AND APPLE SOUP

Use a handheld blender to puree this winning combination of sweet carrots and apples right in the pot. We call for Golden Delicious apples for their consistently good flavor, but feel free to substitute other varieties.

ACTIVE TIME: 20 MINUTES · **TOTAL TIME:** 55 MINUTES
MAKES: 10 CUPS OR 8 FIRST-COURSE SERVINGS

2 TABLESPOONS BUTTER

1 LARGE ONION (12 OUNCES), COARSELY CHOPPED

3 MEDIUM GOLDEN DELICIOUS APPLES (1½ POUNDS)

2 POUNDS CARROTS

2 CANS (14½ OUNCES EACH) GLUTEN-FREE VEGETABLE BROTH, SUCH AS SWANSON BRAND

1 TABLESPOON SUGAR

1 TEASPOON SALT

1 TEASPOON GRATED, PEELED FRESH GINGER

2 CUPS WATER

HALF-AND-HALF OR HEAVY CREAM FOR GARNISH (OPTIONAL)

CHOPPED FRESH CHIVES FOR GARNISH

1 In 5-quart Dutch oven, melt butter over medium heat. Add onion and cook until tender and golden, about 12 minutes, stirring occasionally.

2 Meanwhile, peel apples and carrots. Cut each apple in half and use melon baller to remove core. Cut apples and carrots into 1-inch chunks. Add to Dutch oven along with broth, sugar, salt, ginger, and water; heat to boiling over high heat. Reduce heat to low; cover and simmer until carrots are very tender, about 20 minutes.

3 Remove Dutch oven from heat. Following manufacturer's directions, use handheld blender to puree mixture in Dutch oven until very smooth. Serve soup with a swirl of half-and-half, if you like. Garnish with chives.

EACH SERVING: ABOUT 130 CALORIES | 2G PROTEIN | 23G CARBOHYDRATE | 4G TOTAL FAT (1G SATURATED) | 5G FIBER | 0MG CHOLESTEROL | 795MG SODIUM ☺ ✿ 🍲

FISH STEW

Much like a traditional French bouillabaisse, this light and tasty seafood stew features a delicate fennel flavor and tender pieces of fresh seafood.

ACTIVE TIME: 20 MINUTES · **TOTAL TIME:** 35 MINUTES

MAKES: 4 MAIN-DISH SERVINGS

1   TABLESPOON OLIVE OIL

1   SMALL ONION (4 TO 6 OUNCES), FINELY CHOPPED

1   SMALL RED PEPPER, CHOPPED

1   LARGE GARLIC CLOVE, CRUSHED WITH GARLIC PRESS

½   TEASPOON FENNEL SEEDS

⅛   TEASPOON CRUSHED RED PEPPER

¾   CUP DRY WHITE WINE

1   CAN (28 OUNCES) WHOLE TOMATOES IN JUICE, COARSELY CHOPPED

1   CUP WATER

½   TEASPOON SALT

12   OUNCES COD, HAKE, OR ALASKAN POLLOCK FILLET, CUT INTO 2-INCH PIECES

1   POUND BLUE MUSSELS, SCRUBBED AND BEARDS REMOVED (SEE TIP)

8   OUNCES FRESH OR FROZEN (THAWED) SHELLED AND DEVEINED MEDIUM SHRIMP

½   CUP LOOSELY PACKED FRESH BASIL LEAVES, SLICED

1   In 5- to 6-quart Dutch oven, heat oil over medium heat. Add onion and chopped pepper and cook 6 to 8 minutes or until tender. Add garlic, fennel seeds, and crushed red pepper and cook 1 minute longer, stirring. Add wine; heat to boiling.

2   Stir in tomatoes with their juice, water, and salt; heat to boiling over high heat.

3   Add cod, mussels, and shrimp; return to boiling. Reduce heat to low; cover. Simmer 8 to 9 minutes or until cod and shrimp turn opaque and mussels open. Discard any mussels that have not opened after 9 minutes. Sprinkle stew with basil to serve.

TIP Most markets carry blue mussels. They have bluish-black shells and are harvested wild or cultivated (the cultivated type may not have beards). To debeard a mussel, grasp the hairlike threads with your thumb and forefinger and pull them away from the shell. Once you have removed the beards, cook the mussels within the hour, as they will die quickly and spoil.

EACH SERVING: ABOUT 265 CALORIES | 37G PROTEIN | 15G CARBOHYDRATE | 6G TOTAL FAT (1G SATURATED) | 3G FIBER | 147MG CHOLESTEROL | 805MG SODIUM ☺

HEALTHY MAKEOVER BEEF BURGUNDY

We dropped the bacon—a classic ingredient in a French-style beef stew—but couldn't bear to trade juicy beef chuck for tougher round, even though chuck is a bit fattier. Instead, we added lots more vegetables, like fresh mushrooms, carrots, and frozen peas, to stretch the meat and ramp up the nutritional value.

ACTIVE TIME: 45 MINUTES · **TOTAL TIME:** 2 HOURS 15 MINUTES

MAKES: 8 MAIN-DISH SERVINGS

1 TABLESPOON OLIVE OIL	2 TABLESPOONS TOMATO PASTE
2 POUNDS BONELESS BEEF CHUCK, TRIMMED OF FAT AND CUT INTO 1½-INCH CHUNKS	¾ TEASPOON SALT
	½ TEASPOON COARSELY GROUND BLACK PEPPER
3 LARGE CARROTS (4 OUNCES EACH), CUT INTO 1-INCH PIECES	2 CUPS DRY RED WINE
	4 SPRIGS FRESH THYME
3 GARLIC CLOVES, CRUSHED WITH SIDE OF CHEF'S KNIFE	2 PACKAGES (10 OUNCES EACH) MUSHROOMS, EACH CUT IN HALF
1 LARGE ONION (12 OUNCES), CUT INTO 1-INCH PIECES	1 BAG (16 OUNCES) FROZEN PEAS
2 TABLESPOONS ALL-PURPOSE FLOUR BLEND (PAGE 25)	

1 In 5- to 6-quart Dutch oven, heat oil over medium-high heat until hot. Pat beef dry with paper towels. Add beef, in two batches, and cook 5 to 6 minutes per batch or until well browned on all sides. With slotted spoon, transfer beef to medium bowl. Preheat oven to 325°F.

2 To drippings in Dutch oven, add carrots, garlic, and onion and cook 10 minutes or until vegetables are browned and tender, stirring occasionally. Stir in flour blend, tomato paste, salt, and pepper; cook 1 minute, stirring. Add wine and heat to boiling, stirring until browned bits are loosened from bottom of Dutch oven.

3 Return meat and any meat juices in bowl to Dutch oven. Add thyme and mushrooms; heat to boiling. Cover and bake 1½ hours or until meat is fork-tender, stirring once. Discard thyme sprigs. Just before stew is done, cook peas as label directs. Stir in peas.

EACH SERVING: ABOUT 330 CALORIES | 32G PROTEIN | 26G CARBOHYDRATE | 11G TOTAL FAT (3G SATURATED) | 7G FIBER | 52MG CHOLESTEROL | 475MG SODIUM ☺ ♥ ✿

PORK POSOLE

Posole is made with hominy—dried white or yellow corn kernels with the hull and germ removed. It's a hearty gluten-free ingredient to add to your repertoire. Try it in meatless chili or burritos. This recipe uses canned hominy, which has already been reconstituted.

ACTIVE TIME: 45 MINUTES · **TOTAL TIME:** 2 HOURS 30 MINUTES
MAKES: 10 MAIN-DISH SERVINGS

2 MEDIUM RED PEPPERS	1½ TEASPOONS SALT
3 POUNDS BONELESS PORK SHOULDER, WELL TRIMMED AND CUT INTO 1½-INCH PIECES	½ TEASPOON DRIED OREGANO
	¼ TEASPOON CAYENNE (GROUND RED) PEPPER
1 JUMBO ONION (1 POUND), CHOPPED	1 CUP WATER
4 GARLIC CLOVES, MINCED	1 CAN (30 OUNCES) HOMINY (POSOLE), RINSED AND DRAINED
3 JALAPEÑO CHILES, SEEDED AND MINCED	LIME WEDGES, RADISHES, AND CHOPPED CILANTRO LEAVES FOR GARNISH
1 CUP LOOSELY PACKED FRESH CILANTRO LEAVES AND STEMS, CHOPPED	WARM GLUTEN-FREE CORN TORTILLAS FOR SERVING (OPTIONAL)
2 TEASPOONS GROUND CUMIN	

1 Preheat broiler. Line broiling pan (without rack) with foil. Cut each red pepper lengthwise in half; discard stem and seeds. Arrange peppers, cut side down, in broiling pan. Place under broiler 5 to 6 inches from heat source and broil peppers until charred and blistered, 6 to 8 minutes. Wrap foil around peppers and allow to steam at room temperature until cool enough to handle, about 15 minutes. Turn oven temperature to 325°F.

2 Remove peppers from foil; peel off skin and discard. Cut peppers into 1-inch pieces.

3 In 5-quart Dutch oven, combine roasted peppers, pork, onion, garlic, jalapeños, cilantro, cumin, salt, oregano, cayenne pepper, and water; heat to boiling over high heat. Cover Dutch oven and bake until pork is very tender, about 1 hour 30 minutes.

4 Remove posole from oven; skim and discard fat. Stir in hominy; cover and bake until heated through, about 15 minutes longer. Garnish with lime wedges, radishes, and cilantro. Serve with tortillas, if desired.

EACH SERVING: ABOUT 300 CALORIES | 38G PROTEIN | 14G CARBOHYDRATE | 9G TOTAL FAT (3G SATURATED) | 3G FIBER | 83MG CHOLESTEROL | 565MG SODIUM ☺ 🍲

VIETNAMESE RICE NOODLE SOUP

Although Vietnamese soup is traditionally served with thinly sliced beef, our variation uses rotisserie chicken to create a tasty twist on chicken noodle soup. The rice stick noodles—which are gluten-free—can be purchased in the Asian section of many grocery stores and in Asian markets. For tips on other gluten-free noodles options, see "Gluten-Free Pasta and Noodles," page 111.

ACTIVE TIME: 10 MINUTES · **TOTAL TIME:** 30 MINUTES
MAKES: 7½ CUPS OR 4 MAIN-DISH SERVINGS

4　OUNCES RICE STICK NOODLES (ABOUT ¼ INCH WIDE)

3　GREEN ONIONS

3　CANS (14 TO 14½ OUNCES EACH) LOW-SODIUM GLUTEN-FREE CHICKEN BROTH (5¼ CUPS), SUCH AS SWANSON BRAND

1　CUP WATER

1　PIECE (3 INCHES) FRESH GINGER, PEELED AND THINLY SLICED

¼　TEASPOON CHINESE FIVE-SPICE POWDER

PINCH CRUSHED RED PEPPER

2　CUPS SHREDDED SKINLESS ROTISSERIE CHICKEN MEAT (ABOUT 10 OUNCES)

FRESH HERBS SUCH AS BASIL, CILANTRO, AND MINT, CHOPPED

LIME WEDGES

1　Heat 3-quart saucepan of *water* to boiling over high heat. Remove from heat; add noodles, stirring to separate. Let stand 3 to 6 minutes or until noodles are tender. Drain.

2　Meanwhile, thinly slice green onions diagonally; reserve dark green tops for garnish. In 4-quart saucepan, combine light parts of green onions with broth, water, ginger, five-spice powder, and crushed red pepper; heat to boiling over high heat. Reduce heat to low; cover and simmer 10 minutes.

3　Discard ginger, if you like. Add noodles and chicken; heat to boiling over high heat.

4　Ladle soup into four bowls; serve with herbs, lime wedges to squeeze over soup, and green onion tops.

EACH SERVING: ABOUT 260 CALORIES | 24G PROTEIN | 28G CARBOHYDRATE | 5G TOTAL FAT (1G SATURATED) | 1G FIBER | 63MG CHOLESTEROL | 344MG SODIUM ♥ ♥ ☺ ▤

VALENTINE'S DAY RED CHILI

Beets and fire-roasted tomatoes color this vegetarian chili. Serve with wedges of our Skillet Corn Bread (page 74), if you like.

ACTIVE TIME: 35 MINUTES · **TOTAL TIME:** 1 HOUR 30 MINUTES
MAKES: 9 CUPS OR 6 MAIN-DISH SERVINGS

2   TEASPOONS GROUND CUMIN

1   TEASPOON DRIED OREGANO

½   TEASPOON CHIPOTLE CHILE POWDER

2   TABLESPOONS VEGETABLE OIL

3   LARGE BEETS (6 TO 8 OUNCES EACH), TRIMMED, PEELED, AND CHOPPED

1   JUMBO RED ONION (1 POUND), FINELY CHOPPED

1   LARGE RED PEPPER (8 TO 10 OUNCES), CHOPPED

½   TEASPOON GROUND BLACK PEPPER

4   GARLIC CLOVES, CRUSHED WITH GARLIC PRESS

1   CAN (28 OUNCES) FIRE-ROASTED DICED TOMATOES

1   CAN (15 OUNCES) LOW-SODIUM BLACK BEANS, RINSED AND DRAINED

1   CAN (15 OUNCES) LOW-SODIUM RED KIDNEY BEANS, RINSED AND DRAINED

1   CAN (15 OUNCES) LOW-SODIUM PINTO BEANS, RINSED AND DRAINED

1   CUP WATER

1   CUP REDUCED-FAT SOUR CREAM (CABOT, DAISY, AND BREAKSTONE'S BRANDS ARE GLUTEN-FREE)

¼   CUP PACKED FRESH CILANTRO LEAVES

1   In 7- to 8-quart Dutch oven or heavy saucepot, combine cumin, oregano, and chile powder. Cook over medium heat 1 to 2 minutes or until toasted and fragrant. Transfer to sheet of waxed paper; set aside. In same Dutch oven, heat oil over medium heat until hot. Add beets, onion, red pepper, and ¼ teaspoon black pepper. Cook 15 minutes or until vegetables are tender, stirring occasionally.

2   Add garlic and reserved spice mixture. Cook 2 minutes, stirring constantly. Add tomatoes with their juice, beans, and water. Heat to boiling over medium-high heat. Reduce heat to medium-low and simmer 30 minutes, stirring and mashing some beans occasionally. Season with remaining ¼ teaspoon black pepper. (Can be prepared to this point up to 2 days ahead; transfer to airtight container and refrigerate. Reheat before serving.) Divide among serving bowls and top with sour cream and cilantro.

EACH SERVING: ABOUT 345 CALORIES | 15G PROTEIN | 52G CARBOHYDRATE | 10G TOTAL FAT (3G SATURATED) | 15G FIBER | 13MG CHOLESTEROL | 540MG SODIUM ☺ 🌱 📦

STOVETOP SUPPERS

Dinner on hectic weeknights can be a challenge when you're follow-ing a gluten-free diet. You're tired, harried, short on time, and—most of all—hungry. Dietary restrictions may be the last thing you want to think about. We've got the solution: everyday offerings that you can put together quickly on your stovetop with a minimum of fuss. Our Chicken with Smashed Potatoes, Potpie Style, and Brazilian-Style Pork Chops can be steaming on your plate in just half an hour.

But quick and easy doesn't mean you sacrifice sophistication. The twenty-minute Chicken Tikka Masala delivers a hint of India with its base of basmati rice and flavors such as curry and cilantro. Tangerine Beef Stir-Fry transforms flank steak into a Chinese delight with a quick marinade of fresh tangerine plus garlic, oyster sauce, and ginger. Likewise, gluten-free spaghetti becomes an entirely new dish when you switch out tomato-based pasta sauce for a stir-fry mix of ground chicken with peanut butter, green onions, garlic, and vegetables (see "Gluten-Free Pasta and Noodles" on page 111 for spaghetti options).

When you find yourself longing to just coast through a drive-thru, the high nutritional quality of these recipes may make you think twice. Best of all, after sitting down to one of these satisfying meals, you may even feel less harried.

Spring Vegetable Risotto with Shrimp (page 108)

CHICKEN TIKKA MASALA

Need a quick and flavorful meal? Put this enticing Indian chicken dish and a bowl of basmati rice on the table in just twenty minutes.

ACTIVE TIME: 10 MINUTES · **TOTAL TIME:** 20 MINUTES

MAKES: 4 MAIN-DISH SERVINGS

1   CUP BASMATI RICE

1   TABLESPOON VEGETABLE OIL

1   MEDIUM ONION (6 TO 8 OUNCES), CHOPPED

2   TEASPOONS GRATED, PEELED FRESH GINGER

1   GARLIC CLOVE, CRUSHED WITH GARLIC PRESS

2   TABLESPOONS INDIAN CURRY PASTE (PATAK'S BRAND IS GLUTEN-FREE)

1¼ POUNDS SKINLESS, BONELESS CHICKEN-BREAST HALVES, CUT INTO 1-INCH CHUNKS

¼   TEASPOON SALT

¼   TEASPOON COARSELY GROUND BLACK PEPPER

1   CUP CANNED CRUSHED TOMATOES

½   CUP HALF-AND-HALF OR LIGHT CREAM

¼   CUP LOOSELY PACKED FRESH CILANTRO LEAVES, CHOPPED, PLUS ADDITIONAL FOR GARNISH

1   Prepare rice as label directs.

2   Meanwhile, in 12-inch nonstick skillet, heat oil over medium heat 1 minute. Add onion and cook 6 minutes, stirring frequently. Add ginger, garlic, and curry paste; cook 3 minutes longer.

3   Add chicken, salt, and pepper and cook 2 minutes or until no longer pink on the outside, stirring occasionally. Add tomatoes; cover and cook 3 to 4 minutes longer or until chicken just loses its pink color throughout.

4   Uncover and stir in half-and-half and cilantro. Spoon rice into four shallow bowls; top with chicken mixture and garnish with chopped cilantro.

EACH SERVING: ABOUT 430 CALORIES | 39G PROTEIN | 42G CARBOHYDRATE | 13G TOTAL FAT (4G SATURATED) | 6G FIBER | 93MG CHOLESTEROL | 685MG SODIUM ♥ ☺ ✿

DOES ALCOHOL BELONG
IN THIS PICTURE?

After a hectic day, a quick and easy dinner sometimes calls for a
quicker and easier cocktail. What alcoholic beverages can you serve?
Not beer or malt beverages: They're made with gluten-containing
grains. But wine and distilled liquors, spirits, and cider should not
pose a problem (assuming, of course, you drink in moderation.
That includes everything from absinthe to bourbon, brandy, cognac,
champagne, gin, rum, tequila, vermouth, vodka, whiskey, and more.
Be cautious buying flavored products, however: The flavorings may
not be gluten-free.

CHICKEN AND MUSHROOMS WITH BROWN RICE

Here's a simple and wholesome weeknight meal. Everything—from the chicken to the instant brown rice and veggies—is made in a single skillet.

ACTIVE TIME: 15 MINUTES · **TOTAL TIME:** 45 MINUTES

MAKES: 4 MAIN-DISH SERVINGS

- 2 TABLESPOONS OLIVE OIL
- 1¼ POUNDS SKINLESS, BONELESS CHICKEN THIGHS
- 1 PACKAGE (10 OUNCES) SLICED CREMINI MUSHROOMS
- 2 MEDIUM STALKS CELERY, THINLY SLICED
- 1 TEASPOON CHOPPED FRESH THYME
- 1 CAN (14½ OUNCES) GLUTEN-FREE CHICKEN BROTH (1¾ CUPS), SUCH AS SWANSON BRAND

- 1 CUP INSTANT (10-MINUTE) BROWN RICE
- ½ CUP DRY WHITE WINE
- ¼ TEASPOON SALT
- ¼ TEASPOON COARSELY GROUND BLACK PEPPER
- 8 BABY SUMMER SQUASH, HALVED, STEAMED, AND KEPT WARM, (OPTIONAL)

---

1 In 12-inch skillet, heat oil over medium-high heat until hot. Add chicken and cook, covered, 5 minutes. Reduce heat to medium; turn chicken and cook, covered, 5 more minutes. Transfer to plate.

2 To skillet, add mushrooms, celery, and thyme; cook until vegetables are softened, about 5 minutes, stirring occasionally. Add broth, brown rice, wine, salt, and pepper; heat to boiling.

3 Return chicken to skillet. Reduce heat to low; cover and simmer until juices run clear when thickest part of chicken is pierced with knife and rice is cooked, about 12 minutes. Serve with steamed squash, if desired.

EACH SERVING: ABOUT 340 CALORIES | 35G PROTEIN | 21G CARBOHYDRATE | 13G TOTAL FAT (2G SATURATED) | 3G FIBER | 118MG CHOLESTEROL | 595MG SODIUM ☺

CHICKEN WITH SMASHED POTATOES, POTPIE STYLE

Newsflash, potpie lovers: You can tuck into this comforting rendition, which features potpie filling atop creamy mashed potatoes. Unlike the classic dish, it's 100-percent gluten-free.

ACTIVE TIME: 10 MINUTES · **TOTAL TIME:** 30 MINUTES
MAKES: 4 MAIN-DISH SERVINGS

1½ POUNDS BABY RED POTATOES, EACH CUT IN HALF

1 TABLESPOON VEGETABLE OIL

4 MEDIUM SKINLESS, BONELESS CHICKEN-BREAST HALVES (1¼ POUNDS)

½ TEASPOON SALT

¼ TEASPOON GROUND BLACK PEPPER

2 MEDIUM CARROTS, CUT INTO 2" BY ¼" MATCHSTICK STRIPS (1½ CUPS)

1 CUP GLUTEN-FREE CHICKEN BROTH, SUCH AS SWANSON BRAND

¼ CUP HEAVY OR WHIPPING CREAM

½ TEASPOON DRIED TARRAGON, CRUMBLED

1 CUP TINY FROZEN PEAS, THAWED

1 TABLESPOON BUTTER

FRESH TARRAGON SPRIGS FOR GARNISH (OPTIONAL)

1   In 5-quart Dutch oven, combine potatoes and enough *water* to cover; heat to boiling over high heat. Reduce heat to medium; cover and simmer until potatoes are fork-tender, about 12 minutes.

2   Meanwhile, in nonstick 12-inch skillet, heat oil over medium heat until hot. Add chicken and sprinkle with ¼ teaspoon salt and ⅛ teaspoon pepper; cook 6 minutes. Turn chicken over, cover, and cook until juices run clear when thickest part of chicken is pierced with knife, about 8 minutes longer. Transfer chicken to plate; keep warm.

3   To same skillet, add carrots, broth, cream, and dried tarragon; cover and cook over medium-high heat until carrots are tender, about 5 minutes. Remove skillet from heat and stir in peas.

4   Drain potatoes and return to pot. Coarsely mash potatoes with butter and remaining ¼ teaspoon salt and ⅛ teaspoon pepper.

5   To serve, spoon potatoes onto large platter; top with chicken and spoon vegetable mixture over all. Garnish with tarragon sprigs, if desired.

EACH SERVING: ABOUT 455 CALORIES | 39G PROTEIN | 43G CARBOHYDRATE | 14G TOTAL FAT (4G SATURATED) | 5G FIBER | 110MG CHOLESTEROL | 637MG SODIUM ♥ ❀

HOME-STYLE PAD THAI

Enjoy this takeout classic at home—gluten-free. Our recipe includes both tofu and shrimp, though you can use one or the other, if you prefer.

ACTIVE TIME: 20 MINUTES · TOTAL TIME: 30 MINUTES
MAKES: 4 MAIN-DISH SERVINGS

- 8 OUNCES THIN RICE NOODLES (ABOUT ⅛ INCH WIDE)
- 3 TO 4 LIMES
- 4 OUNCES FIRM TOFU, CUT INTO ½-INCH CUBES (ABOUT ¾ CUP)
- 3 TABLESPOONS REDUCED-SODIUM FISH SAUCE (A TASTE OF THAI AND CHUN'S BRAND MAKE GLUTEN-FREE VERSIONS)
- 2 TABLESPOONS SUGAR
- 8 OUNCES MEDIUM SHRIMP, SHELLED AND DEVEINED
- 2 GARLIC CLOVES, FINELY CHOPPED
- ¼ TEASPOON CAYENNE (GROUND RED) PEPPER
- 2 LARGE EGGS, LIGHTLY BEATEN
- 2 CUPS PACKED THINLY SLICED NAPA CABBAGE (ABOUT 5 OUNCES)
- 1 CUP (3 OUNCES) FRESH BEAN SPROUTS
- ½ CUP LOOSELY PACKED FRESH CILANTRO LEAVES, CHOPPED
- ¼ CUP UNSALTED ROASTED PEANUTS, COARSELY CHOPPED
- 2 TEASPOONS VEGETABLE OIL
- 2 GREEN ONIONS, THINLY SLICED

1 If using rice noodles, soak in large bowl containing enough *hot tap water* to cover. Let stand 20 minutes; drain.

2 Meanwhile, squeeze 2 or 3 limes to make ¼ cup juice; set aside. Cut remaining lime into wedges; set aside. Place tofu between several layers of paper towels and press lightly to drain.

3 In small bowl, combine fish sauce, lime juice, and sugar. Position following items in individual bowls near stovetop: tofu, shrimp, garlic, ground red pepper, eggs, cabbage, bean sprouts, cilantro, and peanuts.

4 In 12-inch skillet, heat oil over medium-high heat until hot. Add tofu, cook 5 minutes or until golden, stirring occasionally. Return tofu to bowl.

5 In same skillet, cook shrimp, garlic, and cayenne pepper over medium-high heat 2 to 3 minutes, stirring until shrimp are no longer pink. Stir in eggs and cook about 30 seconds or until eggs start to set.

6 Add drained noodles, tofu, sliced cabbage, and fish sauce mixture to skillet. Using tongs or two forks, toss to combine, and cook 2 minutes longer. Remove skillet from heat. Add bean sprouts, cilantro, peanuts, and green onions; toss to mix well. Serve with lime wedges and additional fish sauce.

EACH SERVING: ABOUT 495 CALORIES | 20G PROTEIN | 64G CARBOHYDRATE | 19G TOTAL FAT (2G SATURATED) | 3G FIBER | 106MG CHOLESTEROL | 840MG SODIUM

TANGERINE BEEF STIR-FRY

Hassle-free flank steak, sliced into quick-sizzling strips, is the shortcut in this citrus-spiked dish. Marinating the meat in a garlicky ginger-tangerine sauce amps up the Chinese-takeout taste. Serve over hot fluffy white rice or substitute brown rice for more fiber, if you like.

ACTIVE TIME: 30 MINUTES · **TOTAL TIME:** 35 MINUTES
MAKES: 4 MAIN-DISH SERVINGS

1 CUP LONG-GRAIN WHITE RICE	¼ TEASPOON GROUND BLACK PEPPER
2 TANGERINES	1 POUND BEEF FLANK STEAK, CUT IN HALF LENGTHWISE AND THINLY SLICED ACROSS GRAIN
2 GARLIC CLOVES, CRUSHED WITH GARLIC PRESS	
1 TABLESPOON OYSTER SAUCE	2 TABLESPOONS VEGETABLE OIL
1 TEASPOON HONEY	12 OUNCES CREMINI MUSHROOMS, THINLY SLICED
½ TEASPOON GROUND GINGER	12 OUNCES SNOW PEAS
¼ TEASPOON CHINESE FIVE-SPICE POWDER	4 GREEN ONIONS, CUT INTO 1-INCH PIECES
⅜ TEASPOON SALT	

1 Prepare rice as label directs. Meanwhile, with vegetable peeler, remove peel from 1 tangerine in strips. From both tangerines, squeeze ½ cup juice. To large resealable bag, add peel, juice, half of garlic, oyster sauce, honey, ginger, five-spice powder, ¼ teaspoon salt, pepper, and beef. Seal bag and let stand 10 minutes.

2 Meanwhile, in 12-inch skillet, heat 1 tablespoon oil over medium-high heat until hot. Add mushrooms, remaining garlic, and remaining ⅛ teaspoon salt. Cook 3 to 4 minutes or until mushrooms are tender, stirring occasionally. Add snow peas and cook 3 minutes or until snow peas are tender-crisp, stirring occasionally. Transfer to large plate.

3 To same skillet, add remaining oil and heat over medium-high heat until hot. Add beef and marinade; cook 4 minutes or until beef is no longer pink, stirring occasionally. Add mushroom mixture and green onions, tossing to combine. Cook 2 minutes or until green onions have wilted, stirring occasionally. Serve with rice.

EACH SERVING: ABOUT 505 CALORIES | 33G PROTEIN | 58G CARBOHYDRATE | 16G TOTAL FAT (4G SATURATED) | 4G FIBER | 40MG CHOLESTEROL | 415MG SODIUM ♥

SPICED MEATBALLS WITH SAUCY TOMATOES

Easy and fast to prepare, this Middle Eastern–style dish can be served over basmati rice or with toasted gluten-free pitas on the side to scoop up the delectable sauce. The meatballs can be covered and refrigerated overnight before you cook them. If you do this, cook them 5 minutes longer than specified.

ACTIVE TIME: 15 MINUTES · **TOTAL TIME:** 35 MINUTES

MAKES: 4 MAIN-DISH SERVINGS

1 POUND GROUND BEEF CHUCK	½ TEASPOON GROUND BLACK PEPPER
2 GARLIC CLOVES, CRUSHED WITH GARLIC PRESS	1 TABLESPOON OLIVE OIL
5 TABLESPOONS PACKED FRESH PARSLEY LEAVES, FINELY CHOPPED	2 PINTS GRAPE TOMATOES
1 TEASPOON GROUND CUMIN	2 OUNCES FETA CHEESE, CRUMBLED (½ CUP; ATHENOS MAKES A GLUTEN-FREE VERSION)
1 CUP FINELY CHOPPED ONION	BASMATI RICE OR TOASTED GLUTEN-FREE PITAS, FOR SERVING (OPTIONAL)
1½ TEASPOONS DRIED OREGANO	
½ TEASPOON SALT	

1 In large bowl, with hands, combine beef, garlic, 3 tablespoons parsley, cumin, ½ cup onion, 1 teaspoon oregano, salt, and pepper until well mixed.
2 With wet hands, shape mixture into 12 small, slightly flattened meatballs about 2 inches across and 1 inch high.
3 In 12-inch skillet, heat oil over medium-high heat until hot. Add meatballs in single layer. Cook 8 to 9 minutes or until they are browned and instant-read thermometer inserted in center registers 160°F, turning once. Transfer meatballs to plate.
4 Drain fat from skillet and discard. To same skillet, add remaining ½ cup onion; cook over medium-high heat 1 minute, stirring. Add tomatoes and remaining ½ teaspoon oregano. Cook 5 to 7 minutes or until tomatoes soften and some burst, stirring mixture occasionally.
5 To serve, divide meatballs and tomato mixture among serving plates. Sprinkle feta and remaining parsley on top of each. Serve with rice or toasted pitas, if you like.

EACH SERVING: ABOUT 280 CALORIES | 25G PROTEIN | 12G CARBOHYDRATE | 15G TOTAL FAT (7G SATURATED) | 3G FIBER | 84MG CHOLESTEROL | 525MG SODIUM ☺

BRAZILIAN-STYLE PORK CHOPS

This tasty dish is an excellent example of Brazilian cuisine: spicy, with a hint of citrus, and accompanied by black beans.

ACTIVE TIME: 15 MINUTES · **TOTAL TIME:** 30 MINUTES

MAKES: 4 MAIN-DISH SERVINGS

---

4   BONELESS PORK LOIN CHOPS, ¾ INCH THICK (5 OUNCES EACH), TRIMMED

½   TEASPOON GROUND CUMIN

½   TEASPOON GROUND CORIANDER

¼   TEASPOON DRIED THYME

⅛   TEASPOON GROUND ALLSPICE

½   TEASPOON SALT

1   TEASPOON OLIVE OIL

1   ONION, CHOPPED

3   GARLIC CLOVES, CRUSHED WITH GARLIC PRESS

1   CAN (15 TO 19 OUNCES) BLACK BEANS, RINSED AND DRAINED

½   CUP GLUTEN-FREE CHICKEN BROTH, SUCH AS SWANSON BRAND

1   TABLESPOON FRESH LIME JUICE

¼   TEASPOON COARSELY GROUND BLACK PEPPER

¼   CUP PACKED FRESH CILANTRO LEAVES, CHOPPED

FRESH ORANGE WEDGES (OPTIONAL)

1 Pat pork chops dry with paper towels. In cup, mix cumin, coriander, thyme, allspice, and ¼ teaspoon salt. Rub pork chops with spice mixture.

2 Heat nonstick 12-inch skillet over medium heat until hot. Add pork chops and cook until lightly browned outside and still slightly pink inside, about 4 minutes per side. Transfer pork to platter; keep warm.

3 In same skillet, heat oil over medium heat. Add onion and cook, stirring frequently, until golden, about 5 minutes. Add garlic and cook, stirring, 1 minute longer. Add beans, broth, lime juice, pepper, and remaining ¼ teaspoon salt; heat through.

4 To serve, spoon bean mixture over pork; sprinkle with cilantro. Serve with orange wedges, if you like.

EACH SERVING: ABOUT 340 CALORIES | 42G PROTEIN | 25G CARBOHYDRATE | 11G TOTAL FAT (3G SATURATED) | 10G FIBER | 76MG CHOLESTEROL | 760MG SODIUM 💚 😊 🌱

SEARED SCALLOPS WITH TOMATO-OLIVE COMPOTE

Pair sweet scallops and this colorful, savory compote with polenta, a "must-know" gluten-free recipe.

ACTIVE TIME: 15 MINUTES · **TOTAL TIME:** 35 MINUTES
MAKES: 4 MAIN-DISH SERVINGS

2 TABLESPOONS OLIVE OIL	2¼ CUPS BOILING WATER
1 SMALL ONION, CHOPPED	1 CUP LOW-FAT (1%) MILK
1 GARLIC CLOVE, CRUSHED WITH PRESS	¾ CUP YELLOW CORNMEAL (BOB'S RED MILL AND ARROWHEAD MILL'S BRANDS ARE GUARANTEED GLUTEN-FREE)
1 CAN (28 OUNCES) WHOLE TOMATOES	
1 TABLESPOON RED WINE VINEGAR	
¼ TEASPOON GROUND BLACK PEPPER	1¾ TEASPOONS SALT
⅓ CUP KALAMATA OLIVES, PITTED AND CHOPPED	1¼ POUNDS SEA SCALLOPS

1 In 12-inch skillet, heat 1 tablespoon oil over medium heat until hot. Add onion and cook 6 to 8 minutes or until soft and golden, stirring occasionally. Stir in garlic; cook 1 minute. Add tomatoes with their juice, vinegar, and ⅛ teaspoon pepper. Heat to boiling over medium-high heat. Cook 8 to 10 minutes or until thickened, stirring occasionally. Stir in olives and transfer to bowl; cover to keep warm. (Makes 2 cups.)

2 Meanwhile, prepare polenta: In deep 2½-quart microwave-safe bowl or casserole, stir boiling water, milk, cornmeal, and 1½ teaspoons salt. Cover with waxed paper and cook in microwave on High 5 minutes. Remove bowl from microwave and whisk mixture vigorously until smooth (mixture will be lumpy at first). Microwave, covered, on High 2 to 3 minutes longer or until thickened, whisking once after cooking is over. (Makes 3 cups.)

3 Rinse scallops under cold running water; remove and discard tough crescent-shaped muscles. Pat dry with paper towels. Season scallops, on both sides, with remaining ¼ teaspoon salt and ⅛ teaspoon pepper.

4 In clean 12-inch skillet, heat remaining 1 tablespoon oil over medium-high heat until hot. Add scallops and cook 4 to 5 minutes or just until opaque throughout and lightly browned on both sides. Serve scallops with tomato compote and polenta.

EACH SERVING: ABOUT 390 CALORIES | 29G PROTEIN | 38G CARBOHYDRATE | 14G TOTAL FAT (2G SATURATED) | 4G FIBER | 47MG CHOLESTEROL | 1,460MG SODIUM ☻ ☺

SPRING VEGETABLE RISOTTO WITH SHRIMP

Perfect company fare, this medley of asparagus, peas, carrots, and shrimp is as colorful as it is delicious. Arborio rice, a creamy short-grained rice, is the classic choice for risotto. For photo, see page 94.

ACTIVE TIME: 10 MINUTES · **TOTAL TIME:** 35 MINUTES

MAKES: 10 CUPS OR 6 MAIN-DISH SERVINGS

1 CARTON (32 OUNCES) GLUTEN-FREE CHICKEN BROTH, SUCH AS PROGRESSO, PACIFIC NATURAL FOODS, OR IMAGINE BRANDS

1¼ CUPS WATER

½ CUP DRY WHITE WINE

8 OUNCES ASPARAGUS, CUT INTO 1-INCH PIECES

1 TABLESPOON OLIVE OIL

1 SMALL ONION (4 TO 6 OUNCES), FINELY CHOPPED

1 CARROT, PEELED AND FINELY CHOPPED

2 CUPS ARBORIO OR CARNAROLI RICE

1 POUND SHELLED AND DEVEINED LARGE SHRIMP

1 CUP FROZEN PEAS

2 TABLESPOONS FRESH LEMON JUICE

1 TABLESPOON CHOPPED FRESH PARSLEY OR BASIL LEAVES

¼ TEASPOON SALT

¼ TEASPOON GROUND BLACK PEPPER

1 In 2-quart saucepan, heat broth, water, and wine to boiling over high heat. When boiling, add asparagus and cook 2 minutes. With slotted spoon, remove asparagus to small bowl; set aside.

2 Meanwhile, in microwave-safe 4-quart bowl or casserole, combine oil, onion, and carrot. Cook, uncovered, in microwave on High 3 minutes or until vegetables begin to soften. Add rice and stir to coat with oil; cook, uncovered, on High 1 minute.

3 Stir hot broth mixture into rice mixture. Cover bowl with vented plastic wrap and microwave on Medium 15 minutes or until most of liquid is absorbed and rice is tender but still firm, stirring halfway through cooking.

4 Add shrimp, frozen peas, and cooked asparagus; cover and cook in microwave on High 3 to 4 minutes longer or just until shrimp lose their pink color throughout. Do not overcook; mixture will look loose and soupy but will thicken to the proper creamy consistency after cooking.

5 Stir in lemon juice, parsley, salt, and pepper.

EACH SERVING: ABOUT 425 CALORIES | 24G PROTEIN | 67G CARBOHYDRATE | 4G TOTAL FAT (1G SATURATED | 3G FIBER | 115MG CHOLESTEROL | 545MG SODIUM ☺

CARAMELIZED CHILI SHRIMP STIR-FRY

Thanks to a trio of convenient instant ingredients—preshelled shrimp, rice vermicelli, and bagged broccoli, each of which cooks in three minutes—this streamlined seafood stir-fry is ideal on time-is-tight nights. Red pepper flakes add a hit of heat. For photo, see page 2.

ACTIVE TIME: 15 MINUTES · **TOTAL TIME:** 25 MINUTES

MAKES: 4 MAIN-DISH SERVINGS

- 6 OUNCES RICE STICK NOODLES (VERMICELLI)
- 1 POUND BROCCOLI FLOWERETS
- 1 GREEN ONION, FINELY CHOPPED
- ¼ TEASPOON SALT
- 3 TABLESPOONS SUGAR
- 1 TABLESPOON WATER
- 1 TABLESPOON VEGETABLE OIL
- 3 GARLIC CLOVES, VERY THINLY SLICED
- ¼ TEASPOON CRUSHED RED PEPPER
- 1 TABLESPOON LOWER-SODIUM FISH SAUCE (A TASTE OF THAI AND CHUN'S BRAND MAKE GLUTEN-FREE VERSIONS)
- 1 POUND SHRIMP (16 TO 20 COUNT), PEELED AND DEVEINED
- ¼ CUP PACKED FRESH CILANTRO LEAVES
- ¼ TEASPOON GROUND BLACK PEPPER

1 In heavy 12-inch skillet, heat *1 inch water* to boiling over high heat. Add noodles and cook 1 to 2 minutes or until just tender. With tongs, transfer noodles to colander. Rinse under cold water and drain. Leave water-filled skillet on heat.

2 When water in skillet returns to boiling, add broccoli. Cook 3 minutes or until tender-crisp; drain and transfer to large bowl. Toss with green onion and salt. Wipe skillet dry.

3 In same skillet, cook sugar and water over medium-high heat (stirring just until sugar dissolves) 3 to 4 minutes or until mixture turns dark amber. Stir in oil, garlic, and crushed red pepper. Cook 10 seconds, then stir in fish sauce and shrimp.

4 Cook, stirring often, 2 to 3 minutes or until shrimp just turn opaque throughout. Remove from heat and stir in cilantro and black pepper.

5 Divide noodles and broccoli among serving plates. Spoon shrimp with sauce on top of noodles.

EACH SERVING: ABOUT 340 CALORIES | 22G PROTEIN | 53G CARBOHYDRATE | 5G TOTAL FAT (1G SATURATED) | 4G FIBER | 168MG CHOLESTEROL | 600MG SODIUM 💚 ☺

SZECHUAN CHICKEN PASTA WITH PEANUT SAUCE

This ground chicken and mixed veggie pasta features a yummy Asian-style peanut sauce. For pasta options, see "Gluten-Free Pasta and Noodles," opposite.

ACTIVE TIME: 10 MINUTES · **TOTAL TIME:** 25 MINUTES
MAKES: 6 MAIN-DISH SERVINGS

- 1 POUND GLUTEN-FREE SPAGHETTI
- 1 TEASPOON VEGETABLE OIL
- 2 BUNCHES GREEN ONIONS, CUT INTO ½-INCH PIECES
- 1 POUND GROUND CHICKEN OR TURKEY BREAST MEAT
- 2 TABLESPOONS GRATED, PEELED FRESH GINGER
- 3 GARLIC CLOVES, CRUSHED WITH GARLIC PRESS
- 1 TABLESPOON GLUTEN-FREE CORNSTARCH
- 3 TABLESPOONS REDUCED-SODIUM TAMARI, SUCH AS SAN-J BRAND
- ¼ CUP ORANGE JUICE
- 1 BAG (12 TO 16 OUNCES) SHREDDED BROCCOLI, CAULIFLOWER, CARROT, CABBAGE BLEND
- 1 CAN (14½ OUNCES) GLUTEN-FREE CHICKEN BROTH (1¾ CUPS), SUCH AS SWANSON BRAND
- ¼ CUP NATURAL CREAMY PEANUT BUTTER (SEE TIP, PAGE 155)
- HOT PEPPER SAUCE (OPTIONAL)

1 Cook spaghetti as label directs.

2 Meanwhile, in 12-inch skillet, heat oil over high heat. Add green onions and cook, stirring, 1 to 2 minutes or until wilted; transfer to bowl.

3 In same skillet over high heat, cook chicken, ginger, and garlic 3 minutes or until chicken is no longer pink, stirring to break up chicken.

4 In a 2-cup glass measuring cup, whisk together cornstarch, tamari, and orange juice until no lumps remain. Add to skillet along with vegetable blend, broth, peanut butter, and green onions; heat to boiling. Reduce heat to medium and cook 6 to 8 minutes or until vegetables are tender-crisp and sauce thickens slightly, stirring.

5 Drain spaghetti; return to saucepot. Add chicken mixture and toss to combine. Serve with hot pepper sauce, if you like.

EACH SERVING: ABOUT 475 CALORIES | 34G PROTEIN | 70G CARBOHYDRATE | 9G TOTAL FAT (1G SATURATED) | 10G FIBER | 44MG CHOLESTEROL | 580MG SODIUM

GLUTEN-FREE PASTA AND NOODLES

You might assume pasta and noodles are off-limits, but gluten-free pasta products are widely available and can generally be used interchangeably with wheat-containing pastas. Rice pastas are especially popular, in part because their mild flavor goes well with sauce, and they come in a variety of shapes, including the thin Asian rice vermicelli sometimes labeled "rice noodle sticks." You can also find plenty of corn-based and potato-blend pastas. When buying, be mindful of the potential for cross-contamination: Though companies that label their products "gluten-free" tend to be conscientious, they are also unregulated, and there's a risk that products could be manufactured in plants that process gluten-containing grains as well. Ancient Harvest, De Boles, and Tinkyada are a few typically reliable brands. If in doubt, call the company's customer service department for more information.

SPAGHETTI SQUASH "PASTA" PUTTANESCA

This vegetable dish, disguised as a pasta, is a fresh and flavorful gluten-free take on an Italian classic.

ACTIVE TIME: 20 MINUTES · **TOTAL TIME:** 30 MINUTES
MAKES: 4 MAIN-DISH SERVINGS

- 1 LARGE SPAGHETTI SQUASH (4 TO 4½ POUNDS)
- 1 PINT GRAPE OR CHERRY TOMATOES, EACH CUT INTO QUARTERS
- ½ CUP LOOSELY PACKED FRESH BASIL LEAVES, THINLY SLICED, PLUS ADDITIONAL LEAVES FOR GARNISH
- 2 CANS (5 OUNCES EACH) WHITE OR LIGHT TUNA IN WATER, DRAINED AND FLAKED
- ¼ CUP PITTED KALAMATA OLIVES, CHOPPED
- 1 TABLESPOON DRAINED CAPERS, COARSELY CHOPPED
- 1 TABLESPOON OLIVE OIL
- 2 TEASPOON RED WINE VINEGAR
- ½ TEASPOON SALT
- ¼ TEASPOON GROUND BLACK PEPPER
- FRESHLY GRATED PARMESAN CHEESE

1 Place squash in 9-inch glass pie plate and pierce six times with sharp knife. Microwave on High 5 to 6 minutes per pound, about 20 minutes total, or until squash is tender when pierced with knife. Cool 10 minutes for easier handling.

2 Meanwhile, in medium bowl, mix tomatoes, sliced basil, tuna, olives, capers, oil, vinegar, ¼ teaspoon salt, and ⅛ teaspoon pepper until combined.

3 Cut squash lengthwise in half; remove and discard seeds. With fork, scrape flesh to separate into strands and place in large bowl; discard shell. Drain squash if necessary. Add remaining ¼ teaspoon salt and ⅛ teaspoon pepper; toss to combine.

4 Divide squash among four dinner bowls. To serve, top with tomato mixture; garnish with basil leaves and Parmesan.

EACH SERVING: ABOUT 245 CALORIES | 17G PROTEIN | 28G CARBOHYDRATE | 8G TOTAL FAT (2G SATURATED) | 5G FIBER | 24MG CHOLESTEROL | 705MG SODIUM ● ☺ ❀

GRILLED FAVORITES

You may give up a lot of foods on a gluten-free diet, but you can be thankful that meat isn't one of them. In fact, just about anything you can throw on the searing rack of a grill is deliciously fair game for gluten-free eating—and that includes possibilities far beyond steak and chicken. Vegetables taste richer after taking on the charred flavor of flame roasting, in part because fire concentrates their sugars, making them both smoky and sweet—check out our Mexican Veggie Stacks to see what we mean.

This chapter offers plenty of options for meat, fish, and vegetables. Many of our recipes give protein and vegetables space on the grill at the same time. You'll find a number of intriguing approaches to classic grill-worthy meats and seafood. Try the alluring flavor combinations of our Coffee-Spice Chicken with Fruit-Basil Salsa. Burgers take on a new character with ground turkey spiced up with Jamaican jerk seasoning and zesty exclamation points such as thyme, jalapeño, and orange in our Jerk Turkey Burgers. And the flavors of summer will come through loud and clear with Grilled Shrimp, Corn, and Tomato Salad, with corn grilled right on the cob then cut off and combined with poblano chiles and shrimp hot off the grill.

Korean Steak in Lettuce Cups (page 121)

SWEET AND TANGY BARBECUED CHICKEN

It wouldn't be an American summer get-together without barbecued chicken. Our crowd-pleasing recipe precooks the chicken in the oven—so you can make it a day ahead (and not fret about burnt or undercooked chicken). Then, when you're ready to dine, just warm up the chicken on the grill and brush on our luscious gluten-free sauce.

ACTIVE TIME: 25 MINUTES · TOTAL TIME: 2 HOURS
MAKES: 12 MAIN-DISH SERVINGS

3   CHICKENS (4 POUNDS EACH), EACH QUARTERED, SKIN REMOVED

2½ TEASPOONS SALT

2   LEMONS, CUT INTO WEDGES

1   LARGE ONION (12 OUNCES), CUT INTO WEDGES

2   CANS (14½ OUNCES EACH) NO-SALT-ADDED TOMATOES

¼   CUP BALSAMIC VINEGAR

4   TEASPOONS HONEY

4   TEASPOONS SPICY BROWN MUSTARD (HEINZ AND FRENCH'S BRANDS ARE GLUTEN-FREE)

2   GARLIC CLOVES, CRUSHED WITH GARLIC PRESS

1   TEASPOON SMOKED PAPRIKA

2   GALA APPLES, CHOPPED

1   Preheat oven to 425°F. Arrange chicken quarters in large roasting pan (17" by 11½"), overlapping pieces if necessary. Sprinkle chicken with 1½ teaspoons salt; top with lemon and onion wedges. Cover roasting pan tightly with heavy-duty foil. Oven-steam chicken until juices run clear when thickest part of chicken is pierced with tip of knife, about 1¼ hours, turning chicken over halfway through baking time to ensure even cooking. Discard lemons and onion. Refrigerate broth for another use. Transfer chicken to large platter; cover and refrigerate until ready to grill.

2   Meanwhile, prepare barbecue sauce: In 2-quart saucepan, combine tomatoes with their juice, vinegar, honey, mustard, garlic, paprika, 1 teaspoon salt, and apples. Bring to a boil over high; reduce heat to medium and simmer 30 minutes. Puree in blender until smooth. (Makes 4 cups.)

3   Transfer sauce to bowl or, if not using right away, transfer to airtight container. (Sauce will keep, refrigerated, for up to 2 weeks.)

4 Prepare outdoor grill for covered direct grilling over medium heat. Place chicken on hot grill rack over medium heat; cover grill and cook 10 minutes, turning chicken over once. Reserve 3 cups barbecue sauce to serve with grilled chicken. Cook chicken 5 to 10 minutes longer, turning over occasionally and frequently brushing with remaining barbecue sauce until chicken is heated through and sauce is browned. Heat reserved barbecue sauce to serve with chicken.

EACH SERVING: ABOUT 315 CALORIES | 44G PROTEIN | 6G CARBOHYDRATE | 12G TOTAL FAT (3G SATURATED) | 1G FIBER | 135MG CHOLESTEROL | 540MG SODIUM ☺ 🍱

COFFEE-SPICE CHICKEN WITH FRUIT-BASIL SALSA

A jerk-style seasoning of Jamaican allspice and java gives this Caribbean chicken its caffeinated kick. Balancing the heat: a cooling summer salsa of fresh nectarine and juicy watermelon.

ACTIVE TIME: 30 MINUTES · TOTAL TIME: 40 MINUTES

MAKES: 8 MAIN-DISH SERVINGS

3   CUPS SEEDLESS WATERMELON CUBES, CUT INTO ½-INCH CHUNKS (FROM 4-POUND PIECE OF WATERMELON)

1   LARGE RIPE NECTARINE, PITTED AND CUT INTO ½-INCH CHUNKS

3   TABLESPOONS FINELY CHOPPED RED ONION

1   TABLESPOON FRESH LEMON JUICE

2   TABLESPOONS INSTANT UNFLAVORED COFFEE

1   TABLESPOON GRATED, PEELED FRESH GINGER

1   TABLESPOON OLIVE OIL

1¼ TEASPOONS GROUND ALLSPICE

¾   TEASPOON SALT

8   SKINLESS, BONELESS CHICKEN-BREAST HALVES (3 POUNDS)

½   CUP PACKED FRESH BASIL LEAVES, COARSELY CHOPPED

1   In medium bowl, combine watermelon, nectarine, red onion, and lemon juice. Cover and refrigerate while preparing chicken. (Makes 4 cups.)

2   Prepare outdoor grill for covered direct grilling over medium heat.

3   In large bowl, with spoon or fingers, press coffee to pulverize. Add ginger, oil, allspice, and ½ teaspoon salt; stir to combine. Add chicken and toss to evenly coat with spice mixture (you may need to pat mixture onto chicken with fingers).

4   Place chicken breasts on hot grill grate. Cover and cook 8 to 10 minutes or until juices run clear when thickest part of chicken is pierced with tip of knife, turning over once. Transfer chicken to cutting board and let rest 5 minutes. Meanwhile, stir basil and remaining ¼ teaspoon salt into salsa. Slice chicken crosswise and serve with salsa.

EACH SERVING: ABOUT 235 CALORIES | 40G PROTEIN | 8G CARBOHYDRATE | 4G TOTAL FAT (1G SATURATED) | 1G FIBER | 99MG CHOLESTEROL | 310MG SODIUM ☺ ♥

JERK TURKEY BURGERS

When ground turkey is spiced up with Jamaican jerk seasoning and fresh thyme, burger night takes on a juicy and flavorful edge. Gluten-free hamburger buns are available, but you could also choose to serve these spicy patties on the more widely available gluten-free English muffins or wrapped up in gluten-free tortillas.

ACTIVE TIME: 10 MINUTES · TOTAL TIME: 25 MINUTES

MAKES: 4 BURGERS

⅓ CUP REDUCED-FAT MAYONNAISE (HELLMAN'S LITE MAYONNAISE IS GLUTEN-FREE)

2 TEASPOONS CHOPPED FRESH THYME

¼ TEASPOON FRESHLY GRATED ORANGE PEEL

1¼ POUNDS GROUND TURKEY OR CHICKEN

2 GREEN ONIONS, CHOPPED

1 SMALL JALAPEÑO CHILE WITH SEEDS, CHOPPED

¼ TEASPOON SALT

4 TEASPOONS JAMAICAN JERK SEASONING

NONSTICK COOKING SPRAY

4 GLUTEN-FREE MULTIGRAIN HAMBURGER BUNS (SUCH AS RUDI'S BRAND), SPLIT AND TOASTED

LETTUCE LEAVES

1 Prepare outdoor grill for direct grilling over medium heat.

2 In small bowl, stir mayonnaise, thyme, and orange peel until well blended. Set sauce aside. (Makes about ⅓ cup.)

3 In medium bowl, combine turkey, green onions, jalapeño, and salt just until blended. Shape mixture into four ¾-inch-thick burgers. On a sheet of waxed paper, pat jerk seasoning onto both sides of burgers. Lightly spray both sides of burgers with cooking spray.

4 Place burgers on hot grill rack; cook 12 to 14 minutes or until juices run clear when center of burger is pierced with tip of knife, turning over once. (An instant-read meat thermometer inserted horizontally into center should register 170°F.)

5 Serve burgers on buns with lettuce and sauce.

EACH SERVING: ABOUT 415 CALORIES | 30G PROTEIN | 34G CARBOHYDRATE | 19G TOTAL FAT (4G SATURATED) | 2G FIBER | 94MG CHOLESTEROL | 890MG SODIUM ♥ ☺

KOREAN STEAK IN LETTUCE CUPS

No bread required for these wraps. Set out bowls of crisp romaine lettuce, rice, green onions, and sesame seeds and let each person assemble his or her own package. For photo, see page 114.

ACTIVE TIME: 40 MINUTES · **TOTAL TIME:** 55 MINUTES PLUS MARINATING AND STANDING
MAKES: 6 MAIN-DISH SERVINGS

½ CUP REDUCED-SODIUM TAMARI, SUCH AS SAN-J BRAND

2 TABLESPOONS SUGAR

2 TABLESPOONS MINCED, PEELED FRESH GINGER

2 TABLESPOONS SEASONED RICE VINEGAR

1 TABLESPOON ASIAN SESAME OIL

¼ TEASPOON CAYENNE (GROUND RED) PEPPER

3 GARLIC CLOVES, CRUSHED WITH GARLIC PRESS

1 BEEF TOP ROUND OR SIRLOIN STEAK, 1 INCH THICK (1½ POUNDS)

1 CUP REGULAR LONG-GRAIN RICE

¼ CUP WATER

3 GREEN ONIONS, THINLY SLICED

1 TABLESPOON SESAME SEEDS, TOASTED

1 HEAD ROMAINE LETTUCE, SEPARATED INTO LEAVES

1 In large zip-tight plastic bag, combine tamari, sugar, ginger, vinegar, sesame oil, cayenne pepper, and garlic; add steak, turning to coat. Seal bag, pressing out air. Place on plate; refrigerate 1 to 4 hours, turning once.

2 Prepare outdoor grill for direct grilling over medium heat. Just before grilling steak, prepare rice according to package directions; keep warm.

3 Remove steak from bag; reserve marinade. Place steak on hot grill rack over medium heat and grill, turning once, 14 to 15 minutes for medium-rare or until desired doneness. Transfer steak to cutting board; let stand 10 minutes to allow juices to set for easier slicing.

4 In 1-quart saucepan, heat reserved marinade and water to boiling over high heat; boil 2 minutes.

5 To serve, thinly slice steak. Let each person place steak, rice, green onions, and sesame seeds on a lettuce leaf, then drizzle with cooked marinade. Fold sides of lettuce leaf over filling to form a packet to eat like a sandwich.

EACH SERVING: ABOUT 370 CALORIES | 30G PROTEIN | 35G CARBOHYDRATE | 11G TOTAL FAT (3G SATURATED) | 3G FIBER | 69MG CHOLESTEROL | 960MG SODIUM ☺

FLANK STEAK FAJITAS

A garlic rub and lime juice bring out the steak's south-of-the-border side. For tortilla tips, see "Commercial Gluten-Free Breads," page 45.

ACTIVE TIME: 15 MINUTES · TOTAL TIME: 30 MINUTES

MAKES: 4 MAIN-DISH SERVINGS

2   GARLIC CLOVES, CHOPPED

1   POUND BEEF FLANK STEAK

1   BUNCH (10 OUNCES) RADISHES, TRIMMED AND CUT INTO QUARTERS

3/8   TEASPOON SALT

2   LIMES

1/2   CUP REDUCED-FAT SOUR CREAM (CABOT, DAISY, AND BREAKSTONE'S BRANDS ARE GLUTEN-FREE)

8   FAJITA-SIZE (6-INCH) GLUTEN-FREE

TORTILLAS (FOOD FOR LIFE AND LA TORTILLA FACTORY OFFER GLUTEN-FREE VERSIONS)

1/4   TEASPOON GROUND BLACK PEPPER

2   TEASPOONS VEGETABLE OIL

3   POBLANO CHILES, STEMS AND SEEDS REMOVED, THINLY SLICED

1   MEDIUM ONION (6 TO 8 OUNCES), THINLY SLICED

1/4   CUP WATER

1   Rub garlic all over steak; set aside. In small colander or sieve, toss radishes with 1/8 teaspoon salt. Place colander over bowl, cover, and refrigerate. Into small bowl, grate peel from 1 lime and cut lime into quarters; set aside. Stir sour cream into lime peel; cover and refrigerate.

2   Preheat toaster oven to 300°F. Wrap tortillas in foil and heat in toaster oven 15 minutes or until warm and pliable.

3   Heat 12-inch cast-iron or other heavy skillet over medium-high heat until hot. Brush garlic off steak and discard. Squeeze juice from lime quarters all over steak, then sprinkle with 1/4 teaspoon each salt and pepper to season both sides. Add 1 teaspoon oil to skillet, then add steak. Cook 10 minutes for medium-rare, or until desired doneness, turning over once. Transfer steak to cutting board; reduce heat to medium.

4   Add remaining 1 teaspoon oil to skillet and add poblanos and onion. Cook 2 to 3 minutes or until onion is brown, stirring often. Add the water and cook 5 minutes longer or until vegetables are tender, stirring occasionally.

5   Cut steak across grain into thin slices. Cut remaining lime into wedges. Divide steak and vegetables among tortillas; top with lime sour cream. Serve with radish salad and lime wedges.

EACH SERVING: ABOUT 400 CALORIES | 30G PROTEIN | 39G CARBOHYDRATE | 14G TOTAL FAT (5G SATURATED FAT) | 3G FIBER | 86MG CHOLESTEROL | 340MG SODIUM ◔ ☺ ♥

TIPS FOR GLUTEN-FREE GRILLING

Among the considerations worth bearing in mind when you throw your food on the barbecue:

Make sure all marinades are gluten-free, both at home and when you visit a friend's barbecue. Use—or have friends use—separate utensils for gluten-free food.

Take the same precautions with barbecue sauce—or whip up a gluten-free version of your own using the recipe on page 116.

To prevent cross-contamination, grill gluten-free foods first and reserve a portion of the grill for gluten-free foods exclusively. Another option: Cook gluten-free foods on foil to keep them off the grill surface if contaminated food may have been used on it.

For strict gluten-free eating, maintain a grill dedicated to gluten-free foods only, reserving a toaster oven to broil or toast breads or other gluten-containing items. An even better bet: Make your entire barbecue gluten-free. The crowd-pleasing recipes in this chapter will satisfy all your guests.

ANISE STEAK KABOBS

We like to buy a sirloin steak and cut it into chunks to ensure equal-size pieces for even grilling. But, if you prefer, use precut beef cubes from your supermarket for the kabobs. The rub and meat can easily be doubled to feed a larger crowd. Serve with bowls of basmati rice, if you like.

ACTIVE TIME: 10 MINUTES · TOTAL TIME: 20 MINUTES PLUS STANDING

MAKES: 4 MAIN-DISH SERVINGS

1 TEASPOON ANISE SEEDS OR FENNEL SEEDS

2 TEASPOONS OLIVE OIL

½ TEASPOON SALT

¼ TEASPOON COARSELY GROUND BLACK PEPPER

PINCH CRUSHED RED PEPPER (OPTIONAL)

1 BONELESS BEEF TOP SIRLOIN STEAK, 1 INCH THICK (ABOUT 1 POUND), CUT INTO 1¼-INCH CHUNKS

4 (8-INCH) WOODEN SKEWERS

1 Prepare outdoor grill for direct grilling over medium heat.

2 In mortar with pestle or in ziptight plastic bag with rolling pin, crush anise seeds. In medium bowl, combine anise seeds, oil, salt, black pepper, and crushed red pepper, if using. Add beef chunks, tossing until well coated. Cover and let beef stand 10 minutes at room temperature to marinate.

3 Loosely thread meat onto skewers. Place skewers on hot grill rack over medium heat; grill, turning occasionally, 8 to 10 minutes for medium-rare or until desired doneness.

TIP If you like, toss chunks of onion and peppers in a tablespoon of olive oil and thread onto the skewers along with the meat.

EACH SERVING: ABOUT 220 CALORIES | 21G PROTEIN | 0G CARBOHYDRATE | 14G TOTAL FAT (5G SATURATED) | 0G FIBER | 68MG CHOLESTEROL | 340MG SODIUM ✓ ☺ ♥

LIME PORK TENDERLOIN WITH GRILLED PLUMS

For an easy all-on-the grill supper, serve this succulent pork with our shortcut sweet potatoes (see Tip).

ACTIVE TIME: 30 MINUTES · TOTAL TIME: 45 MINUTES
MAKES: 4 MAIN-DISH SERVINGS

1 PORK TENDERLOIN (ABOUT 1¼ POUNDS), TRIMMED

1 LARGE LIME

1 TEASPOON COARSELY GROUND BLACK PEPPER

½ TEASPOON SALT

NONSTICK COOKING SPRAY

4 LARGE PLUMS (ABOUT 1¼ POUNDS TOTAL), EACH CUT IN HALF AND PITTED

1 TABLESPOON HONEY

PINCH GROUND CLOVES

1 Prepare outdoor grill for covered direct grilling over medium heat.

2 Meanwhile, cut tenderloin lengthwise in half. From lime, grate 1 teaspoon peel and squeeze 2 tablespoons juice. In cup, stir lime peel, pepper, and salt; rub mixture on pork. Spray pork with cooking spray.

3 Place pork on hot grill rack over medium heat. Cover grill and cook 2 to 3 minutes, then add plums. Continue grilling 10 to 12 minutes longer, turning both meat and plums once. When done, tenderloin should be brown on outside but still slightly pink in center, and instant-read meat thermometer inserted in thickest part will register 155°F; plums should be browned.

4 Transfer pork and plums to cutting board. Let pork stand 5 minutes to allow juices to set for easier slicing. Cut plums into wedges and place in bowl. Add honey, cloves, and lime juice; toss until coated. Slice pork; serve with plums.

TIP As an accompaniment to the pork, try Shortcut Grilled Sweet Potatoes: Cut 2 medium sweet potatoes into ½-inch-thick slices. Spray both sides with nonstick cooking spray, then sprinkle with ½ teaspoon salt. Place potatoes on microwave-safe plate. Cook in microwave oven on High 5 minutes. Transfer potatoes to hot grill rack and cook, covered, until brown on both sides, about 10 minutes.

EACH SERVING: ABOUT 290 CALORIES | 30G PROTEIN | 23G CARBOHYDRATE | 9G TOTAL FAT (3G SATURATED) | 1G FIBER | 90MG CHOLESTEROL | 351MG SODIUM ☺ ♥

MISO-GLAZED SALMON WITH EDAMAME SALAD

Spread a mixture of miso, ginger, and cayenne pepper on a large salmon fillet. Enjoy with our healthy soybean salad for a Japanese-inspired meal.

ACTIVE TIME: 30 MINUTES · TOTAL TIME: 40 MINUTES

MAKES: 4 MAIN-DISH SERVINGS

EDAMAME SALAD

1   BAG (16 OUNCES) FROZEN SHELLED EDAMAME (GREEN SOYBEANS)

¼   CUP SEASONED RICE VINEGAR

1   TABLESPOON VEGETABLE OIL

1   TEASPOON SUGAR

¾   TEASPOON SALT

⅛   TEASPOON GROUND BLACK PEPPER

1   BUNCH RADISHES (8 OUNCES), EACH CUT IN HALF AND THINLY SLICED

1   CUP LOOSELY PACKED FRESH CILANTRO LEAVES, CHOPPED

MISO-GLAZED SALMON

2   TABLESPOONS WHITE MISO (EDEN BRAND IS GLUTEN-FREE; SEE TIP)

1   GREEN ONION, MINCED

1   TABLESPOON GRATED, PEELED FRESH GINGER

1   TEASPOON BROWN SUGAR

⅛   TEASPOON CAYENNE (GROUND RED) PEPPER

1   SALMON FILLET WITH SKIN ON (1½ POUNDS)

1   Prepare Edamame Salad: Cook edamame as label directs. Drain and rinse with cold running water to stop cooking; drain again. In medium bowl, whisk vinegar, oil, sugar, salt, and pepper until blended. Add edamame, radishes, and cilantro; toss to coat. (Makes about 4 cups.)

2   Prepare outdoor grill for direct grilling over medium-low heat.

3   Prepare Miso-Glazed Salmon: With tweezers, remove any pinbones from salmon. In small bowl, mix miso, green onion, ginger, brown sugar, and cayenne pepper. Rub miso mixture on flesh side of salmon.

4   Place salmon, skin side down, on hot grill rack and grill until just opaque throughout, 10 to 12 minutes, turning once. Serve with Edamame Salad.

TIP Miso, a Japanese culinary mainstay, is made from fermented soybeans. However, whether it's gluten-free or not depends on the koji (yeast-like fermenting agent) that's used. Look for those that use rice- or soybean-based koji (typically this is true of white misos); avoid barley-based versions.

EACH SERVING SALMON WITH 1 CUP SALAD: ABOUT 500 CALORIES | 45G PROTEIN

26G CARBOHYDRATE | 24G TOTAL FAT (3G SATURATED) | 6G FIBER | 80MG CHOLESTEROL

1,470MG SODIUM

GRILLED SHRIMP, CORN, AND TOMATO SALAD

The taste of summer—grilled corn cut straight from the cob, juicy ripe tomatoes, and the incredible flavor of shrimp cooked over the fire.

ACTIVE TIME: 30 MINUTES · TOTAL TIME: 45 MINUTES PLUS STEAMING
MAKES: 4 MAIN-DISH SERVINGS

2 TO 3 LIMES

4 TABLESPOONS OLIVE OIL

¾ TEASPOON SALT

2 PINCHES CAYENNE (GROUND RED) PEPPER

1 TEASPOON GROUND CORIANDER

½ TEASPOON GROUND CUMIN

3 EARS CORN, HUSKS AND SILKS REMOVED

4 RIPE MEDIUM TOMATOES (6 TO 8 OUNCES EACH), EACH CUT IN HALF AND SEEDED

1 POUND LARGE SHRIMP, SHELLED AND DEVEINED, WITH TAIL PART OF SHELL LEFT ON IF YOU LIKE

2 MEDIUM POBLANO CHILES (4 OUNCES EACH)

1 HEAD GREEN OR RED LEAF LETTUCE, THINLY SLICED

1   Prepare outdoor grill for covered direct grilling over medium heat.

2   From limes, grate 1 teaspoon peel and squeeze 3 tablespoons juice. In cup, with fork, mix lime juice with 2 tablespoons oil, ½ teaspoon salt, ½ teaspoon lime peel, and pinch cayenne pepper. Set dressing aside.

3   In medium bowl, with fork, mix coriander and cumin with remaining 2 tablespoons oil, ½ teaspoon lime peel, ¼ teaspoon salt, and pinch cayenne pepper. Brush corn and tomatoes with half of oil mixture. Toss shrimp in oil mixture remaining in bowl.

4   Place corn and whole poblanos on hot grill rack. Cover grill and cook until corn is browned in spots and skin on poblanos is charred and blistered on all sides, 10 to 12 minutes, turning occasionally. Transfer corn to cutting board. Transfer poblanos to large sheet of foil. Wrap foil around poblanos and steam at room temperature 15 minutes.

5   While poblanos steam, place shrimp and tomatoes on hot grill rack (or hot flat grill topper). Add shrimp and cook, covered, just until opaque throughout, 3 to 4 minutes, turning over once. Cook tomatoes until lightly browned, 4 to 6 minutes, turning once. Transfer shrimp to large bowl and tomatoes to cutting board.

6   Remove poblanos from foil. Peel off skins and discard. Cut each poblano lengthwise in half; remove seeds and membranes. Cut poblanos crosswise into thin strips; add to shrimp in bowl. Cut corn kernels from cobs; add to bowl. Peel off and discard skin from tomatoes. Cut tomatoes into thin strips; add to bowl. Add 2 tablespoons dressing to mixture; toss to coat.

7   In another large bowl, toss lettuce with remaining dressing.

8   To serve, place lettuce on platter; top with shrimp mixture.

EACH SERVING: ABOUT 340 CALORIES | 25G PROTEIN | 28G CARBOHYDRATE | 16G TOTAL FAT (2G SATURATED) | 4G FIBER | 180MG CHOLESTEROL | 675MG SODIUM ☺

MEXICAN VEGGIE STACKS

Warm a foil packet of corn tortillas on the grill to make this a full meal.

ACTIVE TIME: 25 MINUTES · TOTAL TIME: 45 MINUTES
MAKES: 4 MAIN-DISH SERVINGS

1 TABLESPOON REGULAR CHILI POWDER	1 MEDIUM ZUCCHINI (10 OUNCES), CUT DIAGONALLY INTO ½-INCH-THICK SLICES
3 TABLESPOONS OLIVE OIL	
¾ TEASPOON SALT	2 LARGE RIPE TOMATOES (10 TO 12 OUNCES EACH), EACH CUT HORIZONTALLY IN HALF
¼ CUP CHOPPED FRESH CILANTRO	
2 TABLESPOONS FRESH LIME JUICE	
1 LARGE POBLANO CHILE (6 OUNCES)	4 OUNCES JALAPEÑO PEPPER JACK CHEESE, SHREDDED (1 CUP; AVOID PACKAGED, PRE-GRATED VERSIONS)
2 EARS CORN, HUSKS AND SILKS REMOVED	
1 LARGE RED ONION (1 POUND), CUT CROSSWISE INTO SLICES	

1   Prepare outdoor grill for direct grilling over medium-high heat.

2   In cup, combine chili powder, 2 tablespoons oil, and ½ teaspoon salt; set chili oil aside. In bowl, combine cilantro, lime juice, and remaining ¼ teaspoon salt and 1 tablespoon oil; set aside.

3   Place poblano and corn on hot grill rack. Grill until poblano is blistered and corn is charred, 10 to 12 minutes, turning occasionally. Remove poblano; wrap in foil and set aside 15 minutes. Transfer corn to cutting board.

4   Push skewer horizontally through each onion slice. Brush both sides of onion and zucchini slices and cut sides of tomatoes with chili oil; place on hot grill rack. Grill onion and zucchini until tender, about 10 minutes, turning over once. Grill tomatoes until slightly softened, 6 to 8 minutes, turning over once. As vegetables are done, remove to platter and keep warm.

5   Unwrap poblano; cut off stem. Cut poblano lengthwise in half; peel off skin and discard seeds, then cut into ¼-inch-wide strips. Cut corn kernels from cobs; add to cilantro mixture.

6   Assemble stacks: Remove skewers from onion slices. On each of four dinner plates, place a tomato half, cut side up; distribute all of zucchini on top of tomatoes, then half of cheese. Arrange onion slice on top of each stack, separating onion into rings; sprinkle with remaining cheese, then with poblano strips. Top with corn mixture.

EACH SERVING: ABOUT 340 CALORIES | 13G PROTEIN | 31G CARBOHYDRATE | 21G TOTAL FAT (8G SATURATED) | 6G FIBER | 30MG CHOLESTEROL | 670MG SODIUM ☺

RATATOUILLE ON THE GRILL

Traditional Provençal ratatouille is a mélange of best-of-summer vegetables slowly simmered in olive oil. Our version is quicker and packs less of a caloric punch, since the veggies are lightly brushed with a vinaigrette mixture, not braised in oil. If you have leftover ratatouille, chop it and toss it with your favorite gluten-free pasta, or layer it between two slices of Homemade Sandwich Bread (page 49), top with some fresh mozzarella, and toast in a panini press or skillet.

ACTIVE TIME: 20 MINUTES · TOTAL TIME: 30 MINUTES

MAKES: 8 MAIN-DISH SERVINGS

- 3 TABLESPOONS RED WINE VINEGAR
- 1 GARLIC CLOVE, CRUSHED WITH GARLIC PRESS
- ¾ TEASPOON SALT
- ¼ TEASPOON COARSELY GROUND BLACK PEPPER
- ¼ CUP OLIVE OIL
- 2 POUNDS PLUM TOMATOES, EACH CUT LENGTHWISE IN HALF
- 2 RED PEPPERS, EACH CUT LENGTHWISE INTO QUARTERS
- 2 MEDIUM ZUCCHINI (8 OUNCES EACH), CUT CROSSWISE INTO ½-INCH-THICK SLICES
- 1 LARGE EGGPLANT (1½ POUNDS), CUT CROSSWISE INTO ½-INCH-THICK SLICES
- 1 LARGE ONION (12 OUNCES), CUT INTO ½-INCH-THICK SLICES
- ½ CUP (LOOSELY PACKED) FRESH BASIL LEAVES, CHOPPED
- 2 OUNCES PARMESAN CHEESE

1   Prepare outdoor grill for covered direct grilling over medium heat.

2   Prepare vinaigrette: In small bowl, whisk together vinegar, garlic, salt, and pepper. In slow, steady stream, whisk in oil until blended.

3   On two jelly-roll pans, lightly brush tomatoes, peppers, zucchini, eggplant, and onion slices with some vinaigrette. With tongs, transfer vegetables to hot grill grate. Cover grill and cook until all vegetables are tender and lightly charred on both sides. Cook tomatoes about 6 minutes; peppers, zucchini, and eggplant about 8 minutes; and onion about 12 minutes. Return cooked vegetables to jelly-roll pans.

4   To serve, on platter, arrange grilled vegetables; drizzle with remaining vinaigrette and sprinkle with basil. With vegetable peeler, shave Parmesan into large pieces over vegetables.

EACH SERVING: ABOUT 155 CALORIES | 4G PROTEIN | 16G CARBOHYDRATE | 10G TOTAL FAT (3G SATURATED) | 5G FIBER | 8MG CHOLESTEROL | 320MG SODIUM ✓ ☺

BAKES & CASSEROLES

Warm your body and soul with richly flavored dinners that may take a little more time but are worth the investment for their substantive and satisfying pleasures. Whether you're cooking up a perfect dinner for two on a leisurely weekend evening, preparing a welcoming meal for treasured friends, or a fixing a homey sit-down with your family, we've got you covered with oven-baked main dishes that will gratify anyone at the table. Don't worry if you're stuck for a side dish: Many of the recipes in this chapter come with gluten-free suggestions for complementary dishes. In the case of Roast Chicken with Winter Vegetables, a savory array of potatoes, carrots, turnips, fennel, and garlic are baked right with the bird.

You'll want a different menu when you're eating with your kids than when you're serving friends, so we've got options for every occasion. Oven-Baked Macaroni and Cheese makes a perfect family meal—and its savory sauce thickened with cornstarch poured over rice noodles keeps the dish gluten-free. For more mature tastes, you've got your pick of delicious dishes, ranging from Oven-Baked Tandoori-Style Chicken to Mushroom-Glazed Pork Chops and Polenta and Spinach Gratin. If you're struggling to maintain your weight on a gluten-free diet, we include recipes that are healthy for reasons that go beyond gluten-free. Our Stuffed Acorn Squash, brimming with a pancetta, pine nut, wild rice, and cannellini bean filling, is a hearty, low-calorie meal in a mostly edible bowl, while Almond-Crusted Tilapia provides a flavorful dinner of lean fish packed with heart-healthy omega-3 fatty acids.

Chicken and Apple Meat Loaves (page 147)

ROAST CHICKEN WITH WINTER VEGETABLES

Take advantage of winter vegetables like turnips, fennel, and potatoes—roasting them with a whole chicken gives them incredible flavor.

ACTIVE TIME: 15 MINUTES · **TOTAL TIME:** 1 HOUR 15 MINUTES
MAKES: 4 MAIN-DISH SERVINGS

1	LARGE ONION (10 TO 12 OUNCES), CUT INTO ½-INCH-THICK SLICES	8	SPRIGS FRESH THYME, PLUS ADDITIONAL FOR GARNISH
1	POUND BABY RED POTATOES, EACH CUT IN HALF OR QUARTERS IF LARGE	7	GARLIC CLOVES, CRUSHED WITH SIDE OF KNIFE, PEEL DISCARDED
1	POUND CARROTS, PEELED AND CUT INTO 2-INCH-LONG PIECES	1	TABLESPOON PLUS 1 TEASPOON OLIVE OIL
2	SMALL TURNIPS (2 OUNCES EACH), PEELED AND CUT INTO 6 WEDGES	⅝	TEASPOON SALT
1	FENNEL BULB (6 OUNCES), TRIMMED, AND CUT INTO 6 WEDGES	⅝	TEASPOON GROUND BLACK PEPPER
		1	CHICKEN (3 TO 3½ POUNDS)

1 Preheat oven to 450°F. In 18" by 12" jelly-roll pan, arrange onion slices in single layer in center. In large bowl, toss potatoes, carrots, turnips, fennel, 4 thyme sprigs, 3 garlic cloves, 1 tablespoon oil, and ¼ teaspoon each salt and pepper until well mixed. Spread in even layer around onion slices in pan.

2 If necessary, remove bag with giblets and neck from chicken cavity; discard or reserve for another use. Rub chicken cavity with ¼ teaspoon each salt and pepper. Place remaining 4 thyme sprigs and 4 garlic cloves in cavity and tie legs together with kitchen string. Rub remaining 1 teaspoon oil on chicken and sprinkle with remaining ⅛ teaspoon each salt and pepper.

3 Place chicken, breast side up, on onion slices in pan. Roast 45 minutes or until juices run clear when thickest part of thigh is pierced with tip of knife and temperature on meat thermometer inserted into thickest part of thigh registers 175°F. Let chicken stand 10 minutes for easier carving.

4 Meanwhile, transfer vegetables around chicken to serving platter, leaving space in center for chicken. Transfer chicken and onion to serving platter with vegetables, tilting chicken slightly as you lift to allow any juices inside to run out into pan. Skim and discard fat from pan juices; pour into small bowl and serve with chicken. Garnish with additional thyme sprigs.

EACH SERVING: ABOUT 555 CALORIES | 45G PROTEIN | 37G CARBOHYDRATE | 25G TOTAL FAT (6G SATURATED) | 7G FIBER | 160MG CHOLESTEROL | 405MG SODIUM

OVEN-BAKED TANDOORI-STYLE CHICKEN

Plain yogurt tenderizes the chicken, while a blend of spices adds heat and exotic flavor.

ACTIVE TIME: 10 MINUTES · **TOTAL TIME:** 40 MINUTES

MAKES: 6 MAIN-DISH SERVINGS

2 TO 3 LIMES

1 CONTAINER (8 OUNCES) PLAIN LOW-FAT YOGURT

½ SMALL ONION, CHOPPED

1 TABLESPOON MINCED, PEELED FRESH GINGER

1 TABLESPOON PAPRIKA

1 TEASPOON GROUND CUMIN

1 TEASPOON GROUND CORIANDER

¾ TEASPOON SALT

¼ TEASPOON CAYENNE (GROUND RED) PEPPER

PINCH GROUND CLOVES

6 MEDIUM BONE-IN CHICKEN BREAST HALVES (3 POUNDS), SKIN REMOVED

1 From 1 or 2 limes, squeeze 2 tablespoons juice. Cut remaining lime into 6 wedges; set aside for garnish. In blender, puree lime juice, yogurt, onion, ginger, paprika, cumin, coriander, salt, cayenne pepper, and cloves until smooth. Place chicken and yogurt marinade in medium bowl or in zip-tight plastic bag, turning to coat chicken. Cover bowl or seal bag and refrigerate chicken 30 minutes to marinate.

2 Preheat oven to 450°F. Arrange chicken on rack in medium roasting pan (14" by 10"). Spoon half of yogurt marinade over chicken; discard remaining marinade.

3 Roast chicken until juices run clear when thickest part of chicken is pierced with tip of knife, about 30 minutes.

4 Transfer chicken to warm platter; garnish with lime wedges to serve.

EACH SERVING: ABOUT 195 CALORIES | 36G PROTEIN | 5G CARBOHYDRATE | 3G TOTAL FAT (1G SATURATED) | 1G FIBER | 88MG CHOLESTEROL | 415MG SODIUM ☺ ♥ 🍱

TURKEY BREAST WITH ROASTED VEGGIE GRAVY

Although we slimmed down this holiday centerpiece by serving a turkey breast without its skin, degreasing the drippings, and thickening the gravy with roasted vegetables, your guests will never know it's healthier! To add a side of roasted Brussels sprouts, see Tip, opposite.

ACTIVE TIME: 40 MINUTES · TOTAL TIME: 2 HOURS 40 MINUTES
MAKES: 8 MAIN-DISH SERVINGS

1 BONE-IN TURKEY BREAST (6 POUNDS)	3 GARLIC CLOVES, PEELED
½ TEASPOON SALT	½ TEASPOON DRIED THYME
¼ TEASPOON GROUND BLACK PEPPER	1 CAN (14½ OUNCES) GLUTEN-FREE CHICKEN BROTH, SUCH AS SWANSON BRAND
2 ONIONS, EACH CUT INTO QUARTERS	
2 STALKS CELERY, CUT INTO 3-INCH PIECES	1 CUP WATER
2 CARROTS, PEELED AND CUT INTO 3-INCH PIECES	

1   Preheat oven to 350°F. Rinse turkey breast inside and out with cold running water and drain well. Pat dry with paper towels. Rub outside of turkey with salt and pepper.

2   Place turkey breast, skin side up, on rack in medium roasting pan (14" by 10"). Scatter onions, celery, carrots, garlic, and thyme around turkey in roasting pan. Cover turkey with loose tent of foil. Roast turkey 1 hour. Remove foil and roast 1 hour to 1 hour and 15 minutes longer. Start checking for doneness during last 30 minutes of roasting. Turkey breast is done when temperature on meat thermometer inserted in thickest part of breast (not touching bone) reaches 165°F and juices run clear when thickest part of breast is pierced with tip of knife. Internal temperature of meat will rise to 170°F upon standing.

3   Transfer turkey to warm platter. Let stand 15 minutes to set juices.

4   Meanwhile, prepare gravy: Remove rack from roasting pan. Pour vegetables and pan drippings into sieve set over 4-cup liquid measure or medium bowl; transfer solids to blender. Let juices stand until fat separates from pan juices, about 1 minute. Skim and discard fat from drippings.

5   Add broth to hot roasting pan and heat to boiling, stirring until browned bits are loosened from bottom of pan. Pour broth mixture through sieve into pan juices in measuring cup.

6 In blender puree reserved solids with pan juices and water until smooth. Pour puree into 2-quart saucepan; heat to boiling over high heat. (Makes about 4 cups gravy.)

7 To serve, remove skin from turkey. Serve sliced turkey with gravy.

`TIP` To roast Brussels sprouts, halve, toss them with with olive oil, salt, and pepper, then roast in a 450°F oven for 18 to 20 minutes, shaking occasionally to prevent them from sticking, until crisp on the outside and tender on the inside.

EACH SERVING TURKEY WITHOUT SKIN: ABOUT 285 CALORIES | 63G PROTEIN 0G CARBOHYDRATE | 2G TOTAL FAT (1G SATURATED) | 0G FIBER | 174MG CHOLESTEROL 255MG SODIUM ☺

EACH ½ CUP GRAVY: ABOUT 20 CALORIES | 1G PROTEIN | 3G CARBOHYDRATE | 0G TOTAL FAT 1G FIBER | 0MG CHOLESTEROL | 125MG SODIUM

HAPPY (GLUTEN-FREE) HOLIDAYS!

Concentrate on hanging the mistletoe: You don't have to plan your holiday dinner menu because we've done it for you using recipes from the pages of this book.

MUSHROOM-GLAZED PORK CHOPS

These golden-crusted chops are quick-seared on the stove, roasted in a roaring oven, and topped with a silky cognac-and-cream sauce.

ACTIVE TIME: 20 MINUTES · TOTAL TIME: 40 MINUTES

MAKES: 4 MAIN-DISH SERVINGS

---

10 OUNCES CREMINI MUSHROOMS, TRIMMED AND QUARTERED

8 OUNCES FRESH SHIITAKE MUSHROOMS, STEMS DISCARDED, CUT INTO 1-INCH PIECES IF LARGE

2 GARLIC CLOVES, VERY THINLY SLICED

1 TEASPOON SUGAR

1 TABLESPOON PLUS 1 TEASPOON SHERRY VINEGAR

½ TEASPOON GROUND BLACK PEPPER

1 TABLESPOON VEGETABLE OIL

4 BONELESS CENTER-CUT PORK LOIN CHOPS (6 OUNCES EACH, 1 INCH THICK)

1 MEDIUM ONION (6 TO 8 OUNCES), FINELY CHOPPED

¼ CUP COGNAC

¼ CUP LIGHT CREAM

½ TEASPOON SALT

2 FRESH SAGE LEAVES, THINLY SLICED

1 Arrange racks in upper and lower thirds of oven. Preheat oven to 450°F.

2 In 15½" by 10½" jelly-roll pan, spread mushrooms in even layer. Sprinkle garlic on top. Roast on upper rack 15 minutes or until mushrooms are tender, juices are released, and garlic is golden brown.

3 Meanwhile, in 9-inch pie plate or other shallow dish, mix sugar, 1 tablespoon vinegar, and ¼ teaspoon pepper. Add pork and turn to evenly coat.

4 Heat 12-inch ovenproof skillet over medium-high heat. Add oil to pan and swirl to coat bottom. When oil shimmers and is almost smoking, add pork. Cook 1 to 2 minutes or until browned; turn pork over and cook 2 minutes longer. Transfer pan to lower oven rack. Roast 7 to 10 minutes or until barely pink in center. Transfer to plate; let rest.

5 To same skillet, add onion. Cook over medium 5 minutes or until browned, stirring occasionally. Add cognac and remaining 1 teaspoon vinegar and cook 30 seconds. Add mushroom mixture with juices; reduce heat to low. While stirring, add cream in slow, steady stream. Stir in salt and remaining ¼ teaspoon pepper. When mixture bubbles, remove from heat.

6 Divide pork chops and their juices among serving plates. Spoon mushroom mixture over pork and garnish with sage.

EACH SERVING: ABOUT 430 CALORIES | 39G PROTEIN | 17G CARBOHYDRATE | 22G TOTAL FAT (7G SATURATED) | 2G FIBER | 127MG CHOLESTEROL | 400MG SODIUM

ALMOND-CRUSTED TILAPIA

Skip the bread crumbs: Here, mild-mannered tilapia is topped with a crunchy coating of almond slices instead. A medley of green beans and mushrooms complete the meal.

ACTIVE TIME: 15 MINUTES · **TOTAL TIME:** 30 MINUTES
MAKES: 4 MAIN-DISH SERVINGS

2 TO 3 LEMONS

2   TABLESPOONS OLIVE OIL

½   TEASPOON SALT

¼   TEASPOON COARSELY GROUND BLACK PEPPER

4   TILAPIA FILLETS (6 OUNCES EACH)

¼   CUP SLICED NATURAL ALMONDS

1   SMALL ONION (4 TO 6 OUNCES), CHOPPED

1   BAG (12 OUNCES) TRIMMED FRESH GREEN BEANS

1   PACKAGE (10 OUNCES) SLICED WHITE MUSHROOMS

2   TABLESPOONS WATER

1   Preheat oven to 425°F. From 1 or 2 lemons, grate 1 teaspoon peel and squeeze 3 tablespoons juice; cut remaining lemon into wedges. In cup, mix lemon peel and 1 tablespoon juice, 1 tablespoon oil, ¼ teaspoon salt, and ⅛ teaspoon pepper.

2   Spray 13" by 9" baking dish with nonstick cooking spray; place tilapia, dark side down, in dish. Drizzle tilapia with lemon mixture; press almonds on top. Bake 15 minutes or until just opaque throughout.

3   Meanwhile, in 12-inch skillet, heat remaining 1 tablespoon oil over medium-high heat 1 minute. Add onion and cook 5 to 6 minutes or until golden, stirring occasionally. Stir in green beans, mushrooms, water, and remaining ¼ teaspoon salt and ⅛ teaspoon pepper. Cook about 6 minutes or until most of liquid evaporates and green beans are tender-crisp. Toss with remaining 2 tablespoons lemon juice. Serve bean mixture and lemon wedges alongside tilapia.

EACH SERVING: ABOUT 315 CALORIES | 33G PROTEIN | 15G CARBOHYDRATE | 15G TOTAL FAT (1G SATURATED) | 5G FIBER | 0MG CHOLESTEROL | 380MG SODIUM ♥ ☺ ♥ ⚘

ROASTED COD WITH POTATOES AND KALE

This good-for-you recipe features lean cod atop a mixture of dark green kale and mashed potatoes.

ACTIVE TIME: 15 MINUTES · TOTAL TIME: 35 MINUTES

MAKES: 4 MAIN-DISH SERVINGS

---

1   PACKAGE (10 OUNCES) FROZEN CHOPPED KALE

1   PACKAGE (16 OUNCES) FROZEN MASHED POTATOES

2   SLICES BACON (SMITH'S, HORMEL, AND OSCAR MEYER OFFER GLUTEN-FREE OPTIONS), CUT CROSSWISE INTO ½-INCH-WIDE PIECES

1   POUND COD OR SCROD FILLET, 1 INCH THICK, CUT INTO 4 PIECES

¼   TEASPOON SALT

2   TABLESPOONS CORNMEAL (BOB'S RED MILL AND ARROWHEAD MILL'S BRANDS ARE GUARANTEED GLUTEN-FREE)

1   LARGE ONION (12 OUNCES), THINLY SLICED

½   CUP GLUTEN-FREE CHICKEN BROTH, SUCH AS SWANSON BRAND

2   TEASPOONS CIDER VINEGAR

---

1 In microwave oven, cook kale, then heat potatoes as package labels direct. Drain kale. In medium bowl, stir kale and potatoes together until blended. Cover and keep warm.

2 Preheat oven to 450°F. Meanwhile, in nonstick 12-inch skillet, cook bacon over medium heat until browned. With slotted spoon, remove bacon to paper towels to drain. Discard bacon fat.

3 On waxed paper, sprinkle cod with salt, then cornmeal, turning to coat. In same skillet, over medium-high heat, cook cod about 2 minutes per side or until lightly browned. Transfer cod to pie plate; place in oven and roast cod 8 to 10 minutes or until opaque throughout. Leave skillet on stove and reduce heat to medium.

4 Add onion to skillet. Cook, covered, 5 minutes or until onion is browned, stirring once. Add broth; cover and cook 4 minutes to wilt onion. Remove from heat; stir in vinegar and bacon.

5 To serve, reheat potato mixture in microwave oven if necessary. Spoon potato mixture onto four dinner plates; top with cod, then onion mixture.

EACH SERVING: ABOUT 315 CALORIES | 28G PROTEIN | 31G CARBOHYDRATE | 9G TOTAL FAT (4G SATURATED) | 5G FIBER | 67MG CHOLESTEROL | 845MG SODIUM ☺ ❀

HOMEMADE PIZZA

This gluten-free pizza crust is crisp and satisfying. Enjoy it with our simple tomato sauce, mozzarella, and basil topping or load it up with broccoli, roasted red pepper, and Kalamata olives, as shown here.

ACTIVE TIME: 35 MINUTES · **TOTAL TIME:** 1 HOUR PLUS RISING
MAKES: 2 PIZZAS OR 8 MAIN-DISH SERVINGS

2½ CUPS ALL-PURPOSE FLOUR BLEND (PAGE 25)

½ CUP BROWN RICE FLOUR

½ CUP MILLET FLOUR

1 TABLESPOON PACKED BROWN SUGAR

1 TABLESPOON XANTHAN GUM (SEE TIP, PAGE 39)

1 PACKAGE QUICK-RISE YEAST

1 TEASPOON SALT

1 CUP VERY WARM WATER (120° TO 130°F)

1 LARGE EGG, AT ROOM TEMPERATURE

2 TABLESPOONS OLIVE OIL

CORNMEAL, FOR SPRINKLING IN PAN

1 CUP MARINARA SAUCE

8 OUNCES FRESH MOZZARELLA CHEESE, THINLY SLICED

¼ CUP FRESH BASIL LEAVES, TORN

1 In food processor, combine flour blend, brown rice flour, millet flour, brown sugar, xanthan gum, yeast, and salt. Process to blend.

2 In 2-cup glass measuring cup, combine warm water, egg, and oil. With motor running, pour into food processor. Process 1 minute. Mixture will be soft and sticky, batter rather than dough. Scrape into medium bowl. Cover with plastic wrap and let stand 15 minutes.

3 Preheat oven to 450°F. Grease two 12-inch cast-iron pans or heavy baking sheets; and sprinkle with cornmeal. Turn dough out onto floured surface and divide in half. Place 1 piece dough in each prepared pan. Using wet hands, press to flatten and spread each into 11-inch circle. Because dough is soft and sticky, rinse hands often. Bake 12 to 14 minutes or until golden brown around edges, rotating pans on oven racks halfway through.

4 Remove crusts from oven and spread with marinara sauce up to ½-inch from edges. Top with mozzarella and other desired toppings. Bake 10 minutes or until crusts brown and cheese melts, rotating pans on oven racks halfway through. Sprinkle with basil.

EACH SERVING: ABOUT 350 CALORIES | 10G PROTEIN | 51G CARBOHYDRATE | 12G TOTAL FAT (5G SATURATED) | 5G FIBER | 46MG CHOLESTEROL | 454MG SODIUM ☺ ♥ ⊛

POLENTA AND SPINACH GRATIN

A creamy spinach topping is layered over slices of ready-made polenta for a comforting side dish or vegetarian entrée (serves 10). You can assemble this casserole completely up to one day ahead, but do not bake it. Cover and refrigerate overnight. Bake in a reheated 425°F oven until hot and bubbly, about 40 minutes.

ACTIVE TIME: 20 MINUTES · **TOTAL TIME:** 55 MINUTES
MAKES: 16 SIDE-DISH OR 10 MAIN-DISH SERVINGS

2	LOGS (24 OUNCES EACH) PRECOOKED PLAIN POLENTA	3½	CUPS WHOLE MILK
2	TABLESPOONS OLIVE OIL	2	TABLESPOONS GLUTEN-FREE CORNSTARCH
1	LARGE ONION, CHOPPED	1	TEASPOON SALT
2	GARLIC CLOVES, MINCED	1	CUP FRESHLY GRATED PARMESAN CHEESE
¼	TEASPOON CRUSHED RED PEPPER		
3	PACKAGES (10 OUNCES EACH) FROZEN CHOPPED SPINACH, THAWED AND SQUEEZED DRY		

1 Preheat oven to 425°F. Cut each polenta log crosswise in half, then cut each half lengthwise into 6 slices. In 13" by 9" ceramic or glass baking dish, place half of polenta slices, overlapping slightly.

2 In 4-quart saucepan, heat oil over medium heat until hot. Add onion and cook until tender and golden, 10 to 12 minutes, stirring occasionally. Add garlic and crushed red pepper and cook 1 minute, stirring. Add spinach and cook 3 minutes to heat through, stirring frequently and separating spinach with fork.

3 In medium bowl, with wire whisk, mix milk and cornstarch. Stir in salt and all but 2 tablespoons Parmesan. Add milk mixture to spinach mixture in saucepan; heat to boiling over medium-high heat. Reduce heat to low; cook 2 minutes, stirring occasionally. Remove saucepan from heat.

4 Spoon half of spinach mixture over polenta slices in baking dish. Repeat layering with remaining polenta slices and spinach mixture. Sprinkle with reserved Parmesan. Bake until hot and bubbly, about 20 minutes.

EACH SIDE-DISH SERVING: ABOUT 155 CALORIES | 8G PROTEIN | 19G CARBOHYDRATE
5G TOTAL FAT (3G SATURATED) | 2G FIBER | 12MG CHOLESTEROL | 625 MG SODIUM

CHICKEN AND APPLE MEAT LOAVES

Easy to prepare chicken meat loaves spiced with fennel seeds, parsley, and brushed with an apple jelly and mustard sauce make for a scrumptious and calorie- and fat-saving main dish. For photo, see page 132.

ACTIVE TIME: 25 MINUTES · TOTAL TIME: 1 HOUR

MAKES: 4 MAIN-DISH SERVINGS

---

1   SLICE GLUTEN-FREE WHOLE-GRAIN BREAD OR HOMEMADE SANDWICH BREAD (PAGE 49)

¼   CUP LOW-FAT (1%) MILK

4   MEDIUM GOLDEN DELICIOUS APPLES

1   POUND GROUND DARK-MEAT CHICKEN

½   CUP FINELY CHOPPED ONION

¼   CUP PACKED FRESH FLAT-LEAF PARSLEY LEAVES, FINELY CHOPPED

1   LARGE EGG, LIGHTLY BEATEN

1½ TEASPOONS FENNEL SEEDS

½   TEASPOON SALT

½   TEASPOON GROUND BLACK PEPPER

1   TABLESPOON VEGETABLE OIL

¼   CUP APPLE JELLY

1   TABLESPOON DIJON MUSTARD (GREY POUPON BRAND IS GLUTEN-FREE)

STEAMED GREEN BEANS, FOR SERVING (OPTIONAL)

---

1   Preheat oven to 450°F. In food processor with knife blade attached, pulse bread into fine crumbs. Transfer to large bowl and stir in milk; let soak. Meanwhile, grate half of 1 apple on large holes of box grater. Cut remaining apple half and 3 whole apples into wedges, removing and discarding cores; set aside.

2   To bowl with crumbs, add chicken, onion, parsley, egg, grated apple, ½ teaspoon fennel seeds, salt, and pepper. With hands, mix until well combined. Divide mixture into 4 equal pieces. On 18" by 12" jelly-roll pan, form each piece into 4½" by 2½" loaf, spacing loaves 3 inches apart.

3   In large bowl, toss apple wedges, oil, and remaining 1 teaspoon fennel seeds; scatter in even layer around meat loaves. Roast 10 minutes.

4   Meanwhile, stir together jelly and mustard until well blended. Brush or spoon thick layer of mixture onto meat loaves. Roast 10 minutes longer or until tops are browned and temperature on meat thermometer inserted into center of loaves registers 165°F. Transfer apples and meat loaves to serving plates. Serve with green beans, if desired.

EACH SERVING: ABOUT 380 CALORIES, 27G PROTEIN | 44G CARBOHYDRATE | 11G TOTAL FAT (2G SATURATED FAT) | 6G FIBER | 145MG CHOLESTEROL | 515MG SODIUM ☺ ❤

LAYERED THREE-BEAN CASSEROLE

This Mexican-inspired vegetarian casserole layers three kinds of beans with corn tortillas, cheese, and salsa.

ACTIVE TIME: 20 MINUTES · **TOTAL TIME:** 1 HOUR 30 MINUTES
MAKES: 6 MAIN-DISH SERVINGS

- 3 POBLANO CHILES
- 1 CUP REDUCED-FAT SOUR CREAM (CABOT, DAISY, AND BREAKSTONE'S BRANDS ARE GLUTEN-FREE)
- ¼ CUP LOW-FAT (1%) MILK
- 9 (8-INCH) GLUTEN-FREE CORN TORTILLAS, SUCH AS CHI-CHI'S OR MISSION BRANDS
- 2 CUPS SALSA VERDE (PACE AND ORTEGA BRANDS ARE GLUTEN-FREE)
- 1 CAN (15 OUNCES) LOW-SODIUM BLACK BEANS, RINSED AND DRAINED
- 6 OUNCES MONTEREY JACK CHEESE, SHREDDED (1½ CUPS; AVOID PACKAGED, PRE-GRATED VERSIONS)
- 1 CAN (16 OUNCES) REFRIED BEANS (ORTEGA AND AMY'S BRANDS ARE GLUTEN-FREE)
- 1 CAN (15 OUNCES) LOW-SODIUM PINK BEANS, RINSED AND DRAINED
- ¼ SMALL RED ONION, VERY THINLY SLICED
- ½ CUP FRESH CILANTRO LEAVES

1 Arrange oven rack 5 inches from heat source. Preheat broiler. In broiling pan lined with foil, arrange poblanos in single layer. Broil 10 to 15 minutes or until blackened all over, turning occasionally to evenly blacken. Wrap peppers in foil; let cool. Reduce oven temperature to 350°F.

2 Meanwhile, in medium bowl, combine sour cream and milk until well blended. In 9-inch square ceramic or glass baking dish, arrange 3 tortillas in single layer, tearing 1 tortilla in half to fit. Peel skin from peppers; discard. Remove and discard stems and seeds; thinly slice peppers.

3 Top tortillas in dish with one-third of salsa, one-third of sour cream mixture, all black beans, one-third of cheese, and one-third of sliced poblanos, in that order, spreading each in an even layer. Repeat layering two more times, with refried beans in center layer and pink beans on top. (Can be prepared to this point up to 1 day ahead; cover and refrigerate.)

4 Place baking dish on jelly-roll pan to catch any drips; bake uncovered 40 to 55 minutes or until bubbly and top browns. Cool in dish on wire rack 10 minutes. Sprinkle with onion slices and cilantro sprigs to serve.

EACH SERVING: ABOUT 490 CALORIES | 24G PROTEIN | 65G CARBOHYDRATE | 16G TOTAL FAT (9G SATURATED) | 12G FIBER | 47MG CHOLESTEROL | 890MG SODIUM

OVEN-BAKED MACARONI AND CHEESE

If you have a hankering for rich, creamy mac and cheese topped with a sprinkling of bread crumbs (and who doesn't?), here's the recipe for you. If you want to get your green veggies all in one convenient dish, try our broccoli variation. For photo, see page 6.

ACTIVE TIME: 25 MINUTES · TOTAL TIME: 1 HOUR
MAKES: 4 MAIN-DISH SERVINGS

- 4 OUNCES EXTRA-SHARP CHEDDAR CHEESE, SHREDDED (1 CUP); AVOID PACKAGED, PRE-GRATED VERSIONS
- 2 OUNCES MONTEREY JACK CHEESE, SHREDDED (½ CUP)
- ¼ CUP GLUTEN-FREE BREAD CRUMBS, PREFERABLY PANKO-STYLE, SUCH AS LE GARDEN BRAND
- 4 TABLESPOONS FRESHLY GRATED PARMESAN CHEESE
- 8 OUNCES GLUTEN-FREE ELBOW MACARONI, PREFERABLY QUINOA PASTA
- 8 OUNCES BROCCOLI FLORETS (OPTIONAL)
- 3 CUPS REDUCED-FAT (2%) MILK
- 1 TABLESPOON PLUS 1 TEASPOON GLUTEN-FREE CORNSTARCH
- ½ TEASPOON DIJON MUSTARD (GREY POUPON AND MAILLE BRANDS ARE GLUTEN-FREE)
- ½ TEASPOON SALT
- ⅛ TEASPOON CAYENNE (GROUND RED) PEPPER
- ⅛ TEASPOON GROUND BLACK PEPPER

1 Preheat oven to 375°F. Grease shallow 2-quart baking dish with nonstick cooking spray. In small bowl, mix Cheddar and Monterey Jack. Measure 1 cup and set aside. Stir bread crumbs and 2 tablespoons Parmesan into cheese mixture in bowl.

2 In large saucepot, cook elbows according to package directions until al dente. If using, add florets to pot 3 minutes before pasta is done. Drain.

3 In same saucepot, whisk milk and cornstarch until smooth. Cook over medium heat, stirring constantly, until mixture thickens slightly and boils. Boil, stirring constantly, 1 minute.

4 Remove pot from heat. Stir in reserved 1 cup cheese mixture, remaining 2 tablespoons Parmesan cheese, mustard, salt, cayenne, and black pepper until cheeses melt. Stir in macaroni. Turn into prepared baking dish and sprinkle with bread crumb mixture. Bake 25 minutes or until casserole is hot and top is lightly browned.

EACH SERVING: ABOUT 500 CALORIES | 22G PROTEIN | 50G CARBOHYDRATE | 22G TOTAL FAT (13G SATURATED) | 3G FIBER | 66MG CHOLESTEROL | 744MG SODIUM

STUFFED ACORN SQUASH

To make this a hearty vegetarian main dish, omit the pancetta. Or serve it as a side with roast turkey or chicken. If you have trouble locating gluten-free pancetta, swap in four slices of cooked bacon, crumbled.

ACTIVE TIME: 35 MINUTES · TOTAL TIME: 55 MINUTES
MAKES: 4 MAIN-DISH SERVINGS

- 2 ACORN SQUASH (1½ POUNDS EACH), EACH CUT IN HALF AND SEEDED
- 1 TEASPOON OLIVE OIL
- 2 OUNCES PANCETTA (BOAR'S HEAD OLD WORLD DELICACIES DICED PANCETTA IS GLUTEN-FREE), FINELY CHOPPED
- 1 SMALL ONION (4 TO 6 OUNCES), FINELY CHOPPED
- 2 LARGE STALKS CELERY, FINELY CHOPPED
- ⅛ TEASPOON CRUSHED RED PEPPER
- ¼ TEASPOON SALT
- ¼ TEASPOON GROUND BLACK PEPPER
- 1 CAN (15 OUNCES) LOW-SODIUM WHITE KIDNEY (CANNELLINI) BEANS
- ¼ CUP WATER
- 1 PACKAGE (7 TO 8 OUNCES) HEAT-AND-SERVE PRECOOKED WILD RICE; DO NOT HEAT
- 4 TEASPOONS PINE NUTS (PIGNOLI)
- ½ CUP PACKED FRESH BASIL LEAVES, THINLY SLICED

1 Preheat oven to 375°F. Line 15½" by 10½" jelly-roll pan with foil. On large microwave-safe plate, arrange squash halves in single layer, cut sides down. Microwave on High 9 to 11 minutes or until knife pierces flesh easily.

2 Meanwhile, in 12-inch skillet, heat oil over medium-high heat until hot. Add pancetta and cook 3 to 4 minutes or until browned and crisp, stirring frequently. With slotted spoon, transfer to paper towels to drain. To drippings in skillet, add onion, celery, crushed red pepper, salt, and black pepper. Cook, stirring frequently, 4 to 5 minutes or until vegetables are tender and golden brown. Remove from heat. In small bowl, mash ¼ cup beans with water. Into vegetables in skillet, stir rice, mashed beans, whole beans, pancetta, 2 teaspoons pine nuts, and half of basil.

3 On prepared jelly-roll pan, arrange squash halves in single layer, cut side up. Divide bean mixture among squash cavities, pressing firmly into cavities and mounding on top. Cover pan with foil. Bake 15 minutes. Uncover and bake 5 to 7 minutes longer or until squash and vegetables are golden on top. Garnish with remaining pine nuts and basil.

EACH SERVING: ABOUT 350 CALORIES | 13G PROTEIN | 59G CARBOHYDRATE | 9G TOTAL FAT (3G SATURATED) | 12G FIBER | 7MG CHOLESTEROL | 330MG SODIUM ☺ ♥ ⊛

SWEET & FRUITY FINALES

No need to deprive yourself of dessert! There are plenty of gluten-free options when it comes to delectable treats—including yummy gluten-free baked goods—and this chapter provides an enticing variety to choose from.

Chocolate, for starters, is naturally gluten-free, although that doesn't make all chocolate products problem-free, and it's wise to exercise caution. For one thing, chocolate is often combined with other ingredients that may not be safe. Another consideration is that chocolate may be processed in plants that also handle gluten-containing products, potentially leading to cross-contamination. When buying chocolate, it's best to give preference to products that are labeled gluten-free. But once you have your chocolate of choice, indulge your sweet tooth with luscious treats like our Drunken Chocolate Figs and Flourless Chocolate-Hazelnut Cake, a gooey gateau that combines melted chocolate and butter with eggs beaten until they triple in volume with a pretty praline candy shard topping. (For baking pointers, see "Gluten-Free Baking Tips," page 24.)

For a fruity turn, satisfy your sweet yearnings with delectable treats like Lemon Meringue Drops that will melt in your mouth and Banana-Berry Parfaits that you can whip up in the time it takes to throw fruit and yogurt into a blender.

If you're hankering for the toothsome satisfaction of a cookie, look no further than Wheat-Free Almond Butter Cookies made with gluten-free flaxseed or our classic Peanut Butter Cookies and Oatmeal-Chocolate Chip Cookies, reworked so they are 100-percent gluten-free.

Flourless Chocolate-Hazelnut Cake (page 162)

OATMEAL–CHOCOLATE CHIP COOKIES

If oatmeal cookies are your favorite cookie jar filler, don't despair: We've created a gluten-free version—studded with chocolate chips—that's as moist and chewy as the classic. However, a small proportion of people with celiac disease cannot tolerate oats, even those labeled gluten-free. So, before you bake up a batch of these cookies, read "The Story of Oats" on page 31 to get the details.

ACTIVE TIME: 30 MINUTES · **BAKE TIME:** 12 MINUTES PER BATCH PLUS COOLING
MAKES: 36 COOKIES

- 2 CUPS ALL-PURPOSE FLOUR BLEND (PAGE 25)
- 1 TEASPOON BAKING SODA
- ½ TEASPOON SALT
- ½ TEASPOON XANTHAN GUM, OPTIONAL (SEE TIP, PAGE 39)
- ¾ CUP BUTTER (1½ STICKS), SOFTENED
- ¾ CUP PACKED BROWN SUGAR
- ½ CUP GRANULATED SUGAR
- 2 LARGE EGGS
- 1 TEASPOON VANILLA EXTRACT (MCCORMICK, SPICE ISLANDS, AND DURKEE BRANDS ARE GLUTEN-FREE)
- 2 CUPS QUICK-COOKING GLUTEN-FREE OATS, SUCH AS BOB'S RED MILL BRAND
- 1 CUP CHOCOLATE CHIPS (NESTLE TOLL HOUSE BRAND IS GLUTEN-FREE)
- 1 CUP WALNUTS, CHOPPED

1 Preheat oven to 375°F. Grease three large baking sheets with nonstick cooking spray (avoid baking spray, which typically contains flour).

2 In medium bowl, whisk together flour blend, baking soda, salt, and xanthan gum, if using.

3 In large bowl, with mixer on low speed, beat butter, brown sugar, and granulated sugar until smooth and fluffy. Beat in eggs one at a time. Beat in vanilla. Beat in flour mixture until blended. Stir in oats, chocolate chips, and walnuts.

4 Drop dough by heaping measuring tablespoons onto prepared baking sheets, spacing cookies 2 inches apart. Bake one sheet at a time for 12 minutes or until cookies are firm and golden brown. Let stand on baking sheet 1 minute before removing with spatula to wire rack to cool completely.

EACH COOKIE: ABOUT 155 CALORIES | 2G PROTEIN | 20G CARBOHYDRATE | 8G TOTAL FAT (4G SATURATED) | 1G FIBER | 21MG CHOLESTEROL | 107MG SODIUM 🍴

PEANUT BUTTER COOKIES

Nothing beats a plate of warm peanut butter cookies with a glass of cold milk. We invite you to sink your teeth into our take on these old-fashioned favorites, made with natural peanut butter and our easy gluten-free flour blend.

ACTIVE TIME: 35 MINUTES · **BAKE TIME:** 12 MINUTES PER BATCH PLUS COOLING
MAKES: 24 COOKIES

---

1 CUP ALL-PURPOSE FLOUR BLEND (PAGE 25)

¼ CUP GLUTEN-FREE CORNSTARCH

1 TEASPOON BAKING POWDER

1 TEASPOON BAKING SODA

½ TEASPOON SALT

1 CUP NATURAL CREAMY PEANUT BUTTER (SEE TIP)

4 TABLESPOONS BUTTER, SOFTENED

½ CUP PACKED BROWN SUGAR

½ CUP GRANULATED SUGAR

2 LARGE EGGS

1 TEASPOON VANILLA EXTRACT (MCCORMICK, SPICE ISLANDS, AND DURKEE BRANDS ARE GLUTEN-FREE)

1 Preheat oven to 350°F. Grease two large baking sheets with cooking spray (avoid baking spray, which typically contains flour). In small bowl, whisk together flour blend, cornstarch, baking powder, baking soda, and salt.
2 In large bowl, with electric mixer on low speed, beat peanut butter, butter, brown sugar, and granulated sugar until smooth and creamy. Beat in eggs one at a time until well blended. Beat in vanilla. Beat in flour mixture.
3 Using heaping measuring tablespoons, shape dough into balls and place 2 inches apart on prepared baking sheets. Press with fork. Bake one sheet at a time for 12 to 15 minutes or until cookies are golden brown at edges. Let stand on baking sheet 1 minute before removing with spatula to wire rack to cool completely.

TIP Choosing natural peanut butter, which is made exclusively from nuts and oil, ensures that the product is gluten-free and avoids added sugar, too. One nationally available brand is Arrowhead Mills. It produces a range of nut butters, from peanut butter to almond and cashew butters, and natural tahini (sesame seed paste).

EACH COOKIE: ABOUT 150 CALORIES | 3G PROTEIN | 17G CARBOHYDRATE | 8G TOTAL FAT (2G SATURATED) | 1G FIBER | 21MG CHOLESTEROL | 188MG SODIUM ♥ ☺ 📦

BUYING GLUTEN-FREE BAKED GOODS

Whether online or in stores, these days you can find a wide variety of gluten-free, ready-made baked goods from cookies to bread. But you can also find gluten-free mixes for brownies, cookies, and cakes from companies such as Betty Crocker to make semi-homemade treats. For a guide to baking mixes chosen by a voting sample of more than 5,000 people, check out the Best of Gluten-Free Winners at TriumphDining.com. Search online for specific items you'd like: You'll find a variety of commercial mixes and recipes that others have had success with, as well as online stores like MyGlutenFree-MarketPlace.com.

CHOCOLATE-HAZELNUT MACAROONS

Chocolate and hazelnut is a delectable flavor combination. Although these chewy-crisp (and gluten-free) cookies are delicious on their own, you can make them even more elegant by sandwiching two together with some melted chocolate.

ACTIVE TIME: 30 MINUTES · **BAKE TIME:** 10 MINUTES PER BATCH PLUS COOLING
MAKES: 30 COOKIES

1   CUP HAZELNUTS
    (FILBERTS; 5 OUNCES)

1   CUP SUGAR

¼   CUP UNSWEETENED COCOA POWDER

1   SQUARE (1 OUNCE) UNSWEETENED
    CHOCOLATE, CHOPPED

⅛   TEASPOON SALT

2   LARGE EGG WHITES

1   TEASPOON VANILLA EXTRACT
    (MCCORMICK, SPICE ISLANDS, AND
    DURKEE BRANDS ARE GLUTEN-FREE)

1   Preheat oven to 350°F. Toast and skin hazelnuts (see Tip). Line two large baking sheets with foil.

2   In food processor with knife blade attached, process hazelnuts, sugar, cocoa, chocolate, and salt until nuts and chocolate are finely ground. Add egg whites and vanilla and process until blended.

3   Drop dough by rounded measuring teaspoons, using another spoon to release dough, 2 inches apart, onto prepared cookie sheets. Bake until tops feel firm when pressed lightly, 10 minutes, rotating cookie sheets between upper and lower oven racks halfway through baking. Cool on cookie sheets on wire racks. Repeat with remaining dough.

TIP Spread the hazelnuts in a single layer on a rimmed baking sheet and toast them in a preheated 350°F oven for 10 to 15 minutes, until any portions without skin begin to brown. Transfer the nuts to a clean, dry kitchen towel and rub them until the skins come off.

EACH COOKIE: ABOUT 60 CALORIES | 1G PROTEIN | 8G CARBOHYDRATE | 3G TOTAL FAT (1G SATURATED) | 0.5G FIBER | 0MG CHOLESTEROL | 15MG SODIUM ☺ ♥ ▤

LEMON MERINGUE DROPS

These melt-in-your-mouth meringues are both crunchy and cloud-light—
and require only five ingredients.

ACTIVE TIME: 45 MINUTES · **BAKE TIME:** 1 HOUR 30 MINUTES PLUS 1 HOUR STANDING
MAKES: 60 COOKIES

---

3   LARGE EGG WHITES

¼   TEASPOON CREAM OF TARTAR

⅛   TEASPOON SALT

½   CUP SUGAR

2   TEASPOONS FRESHLY GRATED LEMON PEEL

1   Preheat oven to 200°F. Line two baking sheets with parchment paper.
2   In medium bowl, with mixer at high speed, beat egg whites, cream of tartar, and salt until soft peaks form. With mixer running, sprinkle in sugar, 2 tablespoons at a time, beating until sugar dissolves and meringue stands in stiff, glossy peaks when beaters are lifted. Gently fold in lemon peel.
3   Spoon meringue into decorating bag fitted with ½-inch star tip. Pipe meringue into 1½-inch stars, about 1 inch apart, on prepared cookie sheets.
4   Bake meringues until crisp but not brown, 1 hour 30 minutes, rotating cookie sheets between upper and lower racks halfway through baking. Turn oven off; leave meringues in oven until dry, 1 hour.
5   Remove meringues from oven and cool completely. Remove from parchment with wide metal spatula. Store in tightly sealed container at room temperature up to 1 month.

EACH COOKIE: ABOUT 5 CALORIES | 0G PROTEIN | 2G CARBOHYDRATE | 0G TOTAL FAT (0G SATURATED) | 0G FIBER | 0MG CHOLESTEROL | 10MG SODIUM ☺ ♥ 📓

WHEAT-FREE ALMOND BUTTER COOKIES

Here's a sweet treat for cookie lovers who are both lactose intolerant and sensitive to gluten. You can find flaxseeds and almond butter in health food stores or in the natural food sections of many supermarkets.

ACTIVE TIME: 10 MINUTES · **TOTAL TIME:** 11 MINUTES PER BATCH PLUS COOLING
MAKES: 36 COOKIES

1 TABLESPOON GROUND FLAXSEEDS OR FLAXSEED MEAL

3 TABLESPOONS WATER

1 CUP SMOOTH ALMOND BUTTER

1 CUP PACKED BROWN SUGAR

1 TEASPOON BAKING SODA

½ TEASPOON VANILLA EXTRACT (McCORMICK, SPICE ISLANDS, AND DURKEE BRANDS ARE GLUTEN-FREE)

PINCH SALT

½ TEASPOON PUMPKIN PIE SPICE (OPTIONAL)

SLICED ALMONDS (OPTIONAL)

1 Preheat oven to 350°F. Line two baking sheets with parchment paper.

2 In small bowl, mix flaxseeds with water. Let stand 5 minutes.

3 In electric mixer, combine almond butter, brown sugar, baking soda, vanilla, salt, soaked flaxseeds, and pie spice if using; mix on low until thoroughly combined. Using tablespoon measure, form dough into balls and place on prepared baking sheets, 1½ inches apart. If desired, top balls with almonds.

4 Bake 11 to 12 minutes or until slightly golden, rotating cookie sheets between upper and lower oven racks halfway through. Cool on rack.

EACH COOKIE: ABOUT 70 CALORIES | 1G PROTEIN | 8G CARBOHYDRATE | 4G TOTAL FAT (0.5G SATURATED) | 13G FIBER | 0MG CHOLESTEROL | 72MG SODIUM ☺ ♥ ◉ ▱

PUMPKIN CRÈME CARAMEL

This showstopping crème caramel is perfect for the holiday table. Since there's no crust, it's 100-percent gluten-free.

ACTIVE TIME: 15 MINUTES · TOTAL TIME: 1 HOUR 5 MINUTES PLUS CHILLING

MAKES: 12 SERVINGS

¼ CUP WATER

1¼ CUPS SUGAR

1 CAN (14 OUNCES) COCONUT MILK (NOT CREAM OF COCONUT), WELL SHAKEN

¾ CUP HEAVY OR WHIPPING CREAM

1 CUP SOLID PACK PUMPKIN (NOT PUMPKIN PIE MIX)

6 LARGE EGGS

2 TEASPOONS VANILLA EXTRACT (MCCORMICK, SPICE ISLANDS, AND DURKEE BRANDS ARE GLUTEN-FREE)

⅛ TEASPOON SALT

FRESHLY WHIPPED CREAM, TOASTED COARSELY SHREDDED COCONUT, AND GRATED NUTMEG

1 Preheat oven to 350°F. In 1-quart saucepan, heat water and ¾ cup sugar to boiling over medium-high heat, stirring to dissolve sugar. Continue to cook, without stirring, 5 to 9 minutes or until caramel is just amber in color. Pour caramel into 9-inch-round, 2-inch-deep ceramic or metal pan, swirling to evenly coat bottom of pan.

2 In 2-quart saucepan, heat coconut milk, heavy cream, and remaining ½ cup sugar just to boiling over medium-high heat, stirring to dissolve sugar.

3 Meanwhile, in large bowl, with wire whisk, mix pumpkin, eggs, vanilla, and salt until blended.

4 Whisk hot coconut milk mixture into pumpkin mixture until blended. Pour pumpkin mixture through sieve into 8-cup glass measuring cup, then into caramel-coated pan. Place pan in roasting pan; place on oven rack. Pour boiling water into roasting pan to come three-quarters of the way up the side of 9-inch pan. Bake 45 to 55 minutes (if using metal pan, start checking for doneness at 35 minutes) or until knife comes out clean when inserted 1 inch from edge of custard (center will still jiggle slightly).

6 Carefully remove pan from water. Allow crème caramel to cool 1 hour in pan on wire rack. Cover and refrigerate overnight or up to 2 days. To unmold, run a small spatula around side of pan; invert crème caramel onto serving plate, allowing caramel syrup to drip down from pan. Garnish with a dollop of whipped cream, coconut, and nutmeg.

EACH SERVING: ABOUT 240 CALORIES | 5G PROTEIN | 24G CARBOHYDRATE | 15G TOTAL FAT (11G SATURATED) | 1G FIBER | 125MG CHOLESTEROL | 70MG SODIUM

FLOURLESS CHOCOLATE HAZELNUT CAKE

You'll love the truffle-like creaminess of this cake, and the hazelnut-praline topping is sure to elicit oohs and ahs. For photo, see page 152.

ACTIVE TIME: 30 MINUTES · **TOTAL TIME:** 1 HOUR 10 MINUTES
MAKES: 12 SERVINGS

- 1 CUP HAZELNUTS (FILBERTS), TOASTED AND PEELED (SEE TIP, PAGE 157), COOLED
- 1¼ CUPS SUGAR
- 8 SQUARES (8 OUNCES) SEMISWEET CHOCOLATE, CHOPPED
- 4 TABLESPOONS BUTTER
- 5 LARGE EGGS
- ¾ CUP HEAVY OR WHIPPING CREAM

1 Preheat oven to 350°F. Lightly grease 9-inch springform pan. Line bottom with waxed or parchment paper; grease paper.

2 In food processor with knife blade attached, place ¾ cup nuts and ¼ cup sugar; pulse until finely ground. Set aside. With chef's knife, roughly chop remaining nuts; set aside.

3 In 3-quart saucepan, melt chocolate and butter over medium-low heat, stirring often. Meanwhile, in large bowl, with mixer on medium-high speed, beat eggs and ½ cup sugar 7 minutes or until tripled in volume. With rubber spatula, fold in chocolate mixture then ground-nut mixture. Pour batter into prepared pan and bake 35 minutes or until top is dry and cracked and toothpick inserted in center comes out slightly wet. Cool in pan on wire rack 10 minutes. Remove side of pan; cool 30 minutes longer.

4 Meanwhile, prepare praline garnish: Line 9-inch cake pan with foil. In pan, spread reserved chopped hazelnuts in single layer. In 12-inch skillet, spread remaining ½ cup sugar in even layer. Cook over medium-high heat 3 to 5 minutes or until sugar is melted and golden amber. Do not stir; swirl sugar in pan to cook evenly. Immediately drizzle melted sugar over nuts to coat evenly. Cool praline completely in pan.

5 While praline cools, in large bowl, with mixer on medium speed, beat cream until soft peaks form, 3 to 5 minutes. To serve, break praline into 12 large pieces. Cut cake and divide slices among serving plates. Top each slice with dollop of whipped cream and shard of hazelnut praline.

EACH SERVING: ABOUT 360 CALORIES | 6G PROTEIN | 33G CARBOHYDRATE | 25G TOTAL FAT (11G SATURATED) | 2G FIBER | 120MG CHOLESTEROL | 75MG SODIUM 🍲

DRUNKEN CHOCOLATE FIGS

Dipped in dark chocolate and drizzled with a made-in-minutes port syrup, fiber-rich fresh figs are swiftly transformed into a simple-meets-sophisticated finale to summer supper.

ACTIVE TIME: 20 MINUTES · **TOTAL TIME:** 25 MINUTES PLUS CHILLING AND STANDING
MAKES: 4 SERVINGS

---

1   CUP RUBY PORT WINE

½   CUP SUGAR

1   CINNAMON STICK

3   SQUARES (3 OUNCES) BITTERSWEET CHOCOLATE

12 FRESH RIPE GREEN OR BLACK FIGS

1 In heavy-bottomed 2-quart saucepan, heat port, sugar, and cinnamon stick to boiling over high heat. Reduce heat to medium and cook 13 minutes, stirring frequently to prevent liquid from boiling over, until syrup is reduced by half. Remove from heat and cool to room temperature (syrup will thicken as it cools).

2 Meanwhile, line cookie sheet with waxed paper. Place chocolate in microwave-safe small bowl or cup and cover with waxed paper. Heat in microwave on High 1 minute or until chocolate is almost melted. Stir until smooth.

3 Holding 1 fig by stem end, dip into melted chocolate, leaving top half uncoated. Shake off excess chocolate. Place chocolate-covered fig on prepared cookie sheet. Repeat with remaining figs and chocolate.

4 Place chocolate-covered figs in refrigerator 15 minutes or until chocolate is set. If not serving right away, refrigerate figs up to 12 hours.

5 To serve, arrange figs on four dessert plates and drizzle with port syrup.

EACH SERVING: ABOUT 350 CALORIES | 3G PROTEIN | 73G CARBOHYDRATE | 8G TOTAL FAT (5G SATURATED) | 7G FIBER | 0MG CHOLESTEROL | 5MG SODIUM 🌱 📦

BANANA-BERRY PARFAITS

This quick dessert looks sensational served in an old-fashioned sundae glass. Because flavored yogurt is sometimes made with gluten-containing additives, we offer simple instructions for flavoring plain yogurt with vanilla.

TOTAL TIME: 10 MINUTES

MAKES: 4 SERVINGS

1¼ CUPS UNSWEETENED FROZEN RASPBERRIES, PARTIALLY THAWED

1 TABLESPOON SUGAR

2⅔ CUPS PLAIN NONFAT YOGURT

1½ TEASPOONS VANILLA EXTRACT (MCCORMICK, SPICE ISLANDS, AND DURKEE BRANDS ARE GLUTEN-FREE)

2 RIPE BANANAS, PEELED AND THINLY SLICED

FRESH RASPBERRIES (OPTIONAL)

1 In food processor with knife blade attached, pulse thawed raspberries and sugar until almost smooth. In a medium bowl, combine yogurt and vanilla to create homemade vanilla yogurt.

2 Into four 10-ounce glasses or goblets, layer about half of raspberry puree, half of yogurt, and half of banana slices; repeat layering. Top with fresh raspberries, if you like.

EACH SERVING: ABOUT 140 CALORIES | 6G PROTEIN | 30G CARBOHYDRATE | 0G TOTAL FAT 2G FIBER | 3MG CHOLESTEROL | 95MG SODIUM 😊 ❤

INDEX

INDEX OF RECIPES BY ICON

This index makes it easy to search recipes by category, including 30 minutes or less, low calorie, heart healthy, high fiber, and make ahead dishes.

♥ HEART HEALTHY

If you're looking for heart-healthy options, here's a list of great choices for every meal. Each main dish contains 5 grams or less saturated fat, 150 milligrams or less cholesterol, and 480 milligrams or less sodium. Each appetizer or side dish contains 2 grams or less saturated fat, 50 milligrams or less cholesterol, and 360 milligrams or less sodium.

☻ HIGH FIBER

Want to get more fill-you-up fiber into your diet? Incorporate the following high-fiber dishes into your regular repertoire. Each contains 5 grams or more fiber per serving.

🍲 MAKE AHEAD

For convenience, you can make all (or a portion) of these recipes ahead of time. The individual recipes indicate which steps you can complete ahead of time, or indicate how long you can refrigerate or freeze the completed dish.

PHOTOGRAPHY CREDITS

James Baigrie: 26, 29, 32, 64, 69, 72, 82, 86, 89, 98, 106, 117, 140
Courtesy of ConAgra: 11 (middle)
Tara Donne: 46
Getty Images: Kathleen Brennan, 23; Crystal Cartier, 19; Comstock, 17;
   Davies and Starr, 9; Brian Hagiwara, 40; Spencer Jones, 11 (top); Joe Vaughn 10 (right)
Brian Hagiwara: 58, 85, 127, 129
iStockphoto: Don Bayley, 22; mustafa deliormanli, 12; DNY59, 11 (bottom);
   Brian Jackson, 15; jsemeniuk, 14; Olga Lyubkina, 45; Neustockimages, 8;
   ranplett, 52; Alberto Tirado 16
Rita Maas: 71
Kate Mathis: 42, 54, 76, 79, 92, 94, 97, 123, 145, 148
Elie Miller: 51, 164
Steven Mark Needham: 156
Ngoc Minh Ngo: 111
Con Poulos: 2, 6, 37, 103, 132, 135, 152
Alan Richardson: 114, 136
Kate Sears: 112, 118, 161
Shutterstock: Dionisvera, 35
Studio D: Chris Eckert, 57; Philip Friedman, 7, 10 (left), 24, 158; J Muckle, 31
Mark Thomas: 63, 75

Front Cover, Spine, Back Cover Top Right: Kate Mathis
Back Cover Top Left, Back Cover Bottom: Con Poulos

METRIC EQUIVALENTS

The recipes that appear in this cookbook use the standard United States method for measuring liquid and dry or solid ingredients (teaspoons, tablespoons, and cups). The information on this chart is provided to help cooks outside the U.S. successfully use these recipes. All equivalents are approximate.

METRIC EQUIVALENTS FOR DIFFERENT TYPES OF INGREDIENTS

A standard cup measure of a dry or solid ingredient will vary in weight depending on the type of ingredient. A standard cup of liquid is the same volume for any type of liquid. Use the following chart when converting standard cup measures to grams (weight) or milliliters (volume).

Standard Cup	Fine Powder (e.g. flour)	Grain (e.g. rice)	Granular (e.g. sugar)	Liquid Solids (e.g. butter)	Liquid (e.g. milk)
1	140 g	150 g	190 g	200 g	240 ml
¾	105 g	113 g	143 g	150 g	180 ml
⅔	93 g	100 g	125 g	133 g	160 ml
½	70 g	75 g	95 g	100 g	120 ml
⅓	47 g	50 g	63 g	67 g	80 ml
¼	35 g	38 g	48 g	50 g	60 ml
⅛	18 g	19 g	24 g	25 g	30 ml

USEFUL EQUIVALENTS FOR LIQUID INGREDIENTS BY VOLUME

¼ tsp	=						1 ml
½ tsp	=						2 ml
1 tsp	=						5 ml
3 tsp	=	1 tbls	=		½ fl oz	=	15 ml
		2 tbls	=	⅛ cup	=	1 fl oz	=	30 ml
		4 tbls	=	¼ cup	=	2 fl oz	=	60 ml
		5⅓ tbls	=	⅓ cup	=	3 fl oz	=	80 ml
		8 tbls	=	½ cup	=	4 fl oz	=	120 ml
		10⅔ tbls	=	⅔ cup	=	5 fl oz	=	160 ml
		12 tbls	=	¾ cup	=	6 fl oz	=	180 ml
		16 tbls	=	1 cup	=	8 fl oz	=	240 ml
		1 pt	=	2 cups	=	16 fl oz	=	480 ml
		1 qt	=	4 cups	=	32 fl oz	=	960 ml
						33 fl oz	= 1000 ml	= 1 L

USEFUL EQUIVALENTS FOR DRY INGREDIENTS BY WEIGHT

(To convert ounces to grams, multiply the number of ounces by 30.)

1 oz	=	¹⁄₁₆ lb	=	30 g
2 oz	=	¼ lb	=	120 g
4 oz	=	½ lb	=	240 g
8 oz	=	¾ lb	=	360 g
16 oz	=	1 lb	=	480 g

USEFUL EQUIVALENTS LENGTH

(To convert inches to centimeters, multiply the number of inches by 2.5.)

1 in =		2.5 cm
6 in = ½ ft =		15 cm
12 in = 1 ft =		30 cm
36 in = 3 ft = 1 yd = 90 cm
40 in =		100 cm = 1 m

USEFUL EQUIVALENTS FOR COOKING/OVEN TEMPERATURES

	Fahrenheit	Celsius	Gas Mark
Freeze Water	32° F	0° C	
Room Temperature	68° F	20° C	
Boil Water	212° F	100° C	
Bake	325° F	160° C	3
	350° F	180° C	4
	375° F	190° C	5
	400° F	200° C	6
	425° F	220° C	7
	450° F	230° C	8
Broil			Grill

THE GOOD HOUSEKEEPING TRIPLE-TEST PROMISE

At *Good Housekeeping*, we want to make sure that every recipe we print works in any oven, with any brand of ingredient, no matter what. That's why, in our test kitchens at the **Good Housekeeping Research Institute**, we go all out: We test each recipe at least three times—and, often, several more times after that.

When a recipe is first developed, one member of our team prepares the dish and we judge it on these criteria: It must be **delicious, family-friendly, healthy,** and **easy to make.**

1.   The recipe is then tested several more times to fine-tune the flavor and ease of preparation, always by the same team member, using the same equipment.

2.   Next, another team member follows the recipe as written, **varying the brands of ingredients** and **kinds of equipment.** Even the types of stoves we use are changed.

3.   A third team member repeats the whole process **using yet another set of equipment** and **alternative ingredients.**

By the time the recipes appear on these pages, they are guaranteed to work in any kitchen, including yours. WE PROMISE.